THEOLOGY
OF THE LIBERATING WORD

THEOLOGY
OF THE LIBERATING WORD

EDITED BY
FREDERICK HERZOG

Abingdon Press
Nashville • New York

ISBN: 0-687-41534-9
Library of Congress Catalog Card Number: 78-141148

SET UP, PRINTED, AND BOUND BY THE
PARTHENON PRESS, AT NASHVILLE,
TENNESSEE, UNITED STATES OF AMERICA

IN MEMORY OF KARL BARTH

1886-1968

FOREWORD

The dynamics of the American cultural process have recently begun to focus on the issue of liberation. However embryonic, these essays intimate through which bottleneck we have to pass in order to move toward *liberation theology*.

In no wise is this book offered to the reader on the premise that American theology should learn another lesson yet from German theology. Times are too filled with horror and the world has shrunk too much that we could still afford to think in terms of one theological nationalism besting another and serving as its model. Rather, the widespread conflict in the church compels us to discover the confluence of theological issues the world over.

Theology has as its source the biblical message. If it there finds the Word that liberates, it might again speak credibly of freedom for our time. Theology must ask whether today it is taking this Word seriously at all. The Word is not a straitjacket, but the *creator* of freedom—of new possibilities of life. These essays (by no means completely homogeneous in outlook!) are an invitation to search anew for the creativity of the Word. In the process we may find that theology's present task is the christianization of the church (in the spirit of Kierkegaard)—after its total secularization.

The anxiety of many over the new conflict in the church may be due partly to no more than sudden painful disillusionment over liberalism's optimistic view of man. The Word makes us discover a new realism as it confronts us with man's imperfection and the consequent appearance of the *ecclesia militans*.

I wish to thank those who have unstintingly offered their assistance as editorial council for the volume: Brevard S. Childs, John Macquarrie, and Roger L. Shinn. Jürgen Moltmann served as editorial liaison with *Evangelische Theologie*. My Duke colleague Orval S. Wintermute helped in the editing of the Kraus manuscript. And my wife, Kristin, worked hard at the tedious job of "editorial assistant."

R. Dick Johns, M. Douglas Meeks, Robert T. Osborn, and Reinhard Ulrich are due a special word of thanks for making lucid difficult Teutonic language.

The reader, I am sure, would like to know that Eberhard Jüngel teaches at the University of Tübingen, Hans-Dieter Bastian at the teachers' college in Bonn, and Hans-Joachim Kraus as well as Hans Conzelmann at the University of Göttingen.

Without the interest and cooperation of Ernst Wolf, editor of *Evangelische Theologie*, the present volume would not have been possible. We are greatly in his debt.

FREDERICK HERZOG

CONTENTS

INTRODUCTION:
A NEW CHURCH CONFLICT?

FREDERICK HERZOG

"Much of our tradition-bound speech is structured in a way that creates a polarity between us and everyone (and everything) else. Our language forces us to conceive so much of life as an endless, goal-focused struggle, a war. And success, in even the most mild endeavors, is depicted in outright battlefield terminology: We grapple with, strive, clash, cross swords, lock horns, tussle, contend, engage, fight for or take the offensive to achieve (with flying colors) a triumph, victory, conquest, a win, a mastery, a put-down, a killing, etc. . . . . Thus, at a time when we need to be dismantling barriers to human unity, we continue to generate tension as we talk—and our talk, in turn, influences our behavior." [1] There is a great yearning among men today everywhere that we overcome the tensions that haunt our sleeping as well as our waking hours. Especially young people are turned off by anyone who speaks of conflict. Yet the fact remains that we live in a world in which conflict is real. Ultimately it relates to human nature that men do not escape conflict.[2] The church has not been exempt

[1] William Hedgepath, "We Need New Ways to Say What's Real," *Look,* 34:1 (January 13, 1970), p. 48.

[2] Cf. Reinhold Niebuhr, *Moral Man and Immoral Society* (New York, 1932), p. xxiii: "Whatever increase in social intelligence and moral goodwill may be achieved in human history, may serve to mitigate the brutalities of social conflict, but they cannot abolish the conflict itself."

from this aspect of the human condition. The fact found its time-honored expression in the phrase *ecclesia militans.*

As one looks back upon church history there seems to have been no time when there was no conflict in the church. Occasionally it has been covert. But the major incisions in church history have been marked by major overt conflict. So it was at the time of the Reformation, or, more recently, in the struggle of the Confessing Church against the "German Christians" during the Hitler Reich of 1933-1945. The conflict has often been less encompassing and yet nonetheless real. So, for example, in the work of Kierkegaard.

Usually the conflict boils down to the question of the loss of the substance of the Christian faith. Dare the Christian faith enter an alliance with culture, or with the state? May the Christian faith merge with secularity or join with other faiths? There was always conflict in the church where there was a question about the integrity of the substance of the faith. But what makes a person think there is such a thing as the substance of the faith? Here the question of authority enters the picture.

The New Authority Conflict

The issue of whether there is a substance of the faith we dare not lose does not emerge in every age the same way. Luther faced a different situation from Athanasius, Bonhoeffer a different one from Kierkegaard. Today we are caught between a Christian romanticism and a Christian legalism. Christian romanticism takes many forms, radicalism, liberalism, secularism, etc. Today it has a strangely utopian note: "We are marching to euphoria, euphoria. . . ." A recent *Time* essay on "Changing Theologies for a Changing World" moves in this direction, partly misrepresenting the intentions of some of the theologians to which it appeals.[3] Christian romanticism does not take man's self-contradiction into account. It generally gives the impression that most of man's problems are soluable and that he is not really caught in a dilemma. Christian realism tries to acknowledge the compromise that takes place in the process.[4]

Beside a Christian romanticism that sees life through rose-colored glasses a new Christian legalism is gaining ground. "Law and order" is a demand of countless religious people who are afraid of the rapid changes that Christian romanticists are sanctioning or effectively initiating themselves.

One group is asking the other: With what right are you demanding law and order? What entitles you to call for revolution? It is in the conflict between these two groups that the present authority problem emerges. What

[3] *Time* (December 26, 1969), p. 42.
[4] *Time* (December 5, 1969), p. 26.

authorizes one position over the other? Or, what authorizes any Christian position in the first place, so that the substance of the faith is retained?

Obviously the authority problem concerns not merely attitudes or ideologies. It breaks down into concrete situations to which we must address ourselves. The ideologies in the church are in conflict over many concrete problems. Basically they all relate to the issue of acculturation.

It is impossible for the Christian faith not to become part of culture. But it is always a question of whether this will become a matter of the liberation of or the accommodation to culture. By and large it is *culture-accommodation* that accounts for the conflict in the American churches today. It is generally understood that they are more an expression of culture-religion than of covenant-community. One need only point to segregation in the church, which is not merely a problem of the South. The church does what society demands and becomes a tool in the hands of security-anxious men who desire sanctions for their mores. One can easily draw parallels between our situation and that of Hitler's Germany, as George Shriver recently has pointed out with respect to the South: "The Bible-belt south has been described as, in general, theologically conservative or even partly fundamentalistic and as opposed to theological liberalism. But that same south has practiced the crassest form of liberalism; namely, a culture-accommodation as complete as that of the 'German Christians.' " [5] What is at stake is the question of the center of loyalty in society. Just whom does American man worship? Who calls forth man's obedience? From the wide spectrum of issues we shall select only a few that focus the problem of accommodation.

(1) *Throne and Altar.* Recently the discussion of President Nixon's White House worship services revealed a specific aspect of culture-accommodation that quite openly demonstrates the authority problem. Reinhold Niebuhr argued the case against the use of White House premises for worship services on grounds of the First Amendment. But what of Christian authority for or against the president of the United States using the religious establishment for his private edification? [6] All the questions signified by the American flag in the churches and chaplains in the military fall into the same category and call for review.

(2) *Creeping Fascism.* Political pressure on the opposition in this country

[5] George H. Shriver, "When Conservatism Is Liberalism," *The Christian Century* (August 6, 1969), p. 1041. It is surprising to see how many parallels today are being drawn between the present American situation and the German situation of the Hitler Reich. One further example: Hubert Locke reflecting on his "deep-rooted conviction that America in the 1960's and '70s is going through the same experience as Germany in the 1930's and 1940's." Quoted in "Church Dangers Tied to Nazi Germany," *Christian Advocate*, 14:8 (April 16, 1970), p. 3.

[6] In view of what "the silent majority" thinks about these matters, a radical assessment from the theological perspective is all the more called for. Cf. the editorial "Worship Services at White House," *Durham Morning Herald* (August 19, 1969), p. 4.

by "effete snob" speeches, attacks upon news media, and increasing official sanction of right-wing movements needs to be viewed also from the perspective of how much of this is done under the aegis of a civil religion that does not really know what it means to be self-critical.[7]

(3) *Racism.* The increasing tensions between black and white are part and parcel of the great authority problem arising in the conflicts of American society. Recently attempts have been made to justify black revolutionary action from the Christian perspective on several grounds. For example, James H. Cone writes: "To put it simply, Black Theology knows no authority more binding than the experience of oppression itself. . . . Concretely, this means that Black Theology is not prepared to accept any doctrine of God, Christ, or Scripture which contradicts the black demand for freedom now." [8] Just how much is Black Theology repeating the white experience? Who is giving anyone the right to make his experience ultimate authority, regardless of how much on top of the world he feels or how hard pressed he is?

(4) At the same time the *Vietnam War* continues. And the question of how to "live with the war" becomes for many more and more an either/or question. Can one continue to live in America? Must one not go to prison or emigrate? These are no longer academic questions.[9]

(5) *The Drug Syndrome.* Doubtless the pressures of these unresolved conflicts are felt especially by the young people. There are many who valiantly fight the revolutionary battle. But there are untold thousands and hundred thousands more who drop out and take drugs, LSD, heroin, or whatever is handy. The problem has taken on epidemic proportions, as everyone knows. The U.S. government is ready to put up thirty million dollars to fight it. Why mention the authority problem here? Said a fourteen-year-old girl, a heroin addict: "After I got involved, I used to see my father, but my father wouldn't say anything. My mother used to lay down a few rules. I talked to them about it. I used to go and tell my mother, kind of hoping that she'd say to me, 'Stop and that's final.' But she never did." [10] Can society still offer a center of loyalty to parents and children in the increasing dilemmas of aimless youth that sees no point in playing along in the games of the consumer society?

[7] Cf. David Shaffer, "The Danger of Fascism," *The Duke Chronicle* (October 30, 1969), p. 4.

[8] James H. Cone, *Black Theology and Black Power* (New York, 1969), p. 120. In my opinion, the emergence of black theology is the most important event of the sixties in American theology. An acknowledgment of the achievement, however, does not imply that we should forego critical dialogue. Cf. my essay: "God: Black or White? The Upshot of the Debate About God in the Sixties," *Review and Expositor*, 67:3 (Summer, 1970), pp. 299-313.

[9] See Carl L. Kline, "Why We Moved to Canada," *Fellowship*, 35:11 (November, 1969), pp. 26-27.

[10] *Time* (March 16, 1970), p. 17.

One of the characteristics of our present situation is that, while the conflict situation is sensed, the real problem has not been nailed down as yet. Jeffrey K. Hadden's recent sociological analysis of *The Gathering Storm in the Churches* comes as close to grasping what is at stake as any examination of the situation I know. Hadden believes that many church leaders and Christians have been concerned about unifying the church while turning *"their backs on other developments which . . . are threatening seriously to disrupt or alter existing church structures."* [11] Central to Hadden's thesis is the view *"that the Protestant churches are involved in a deep and entangling crisis which in the years ahead may seriously disrupt or alter the very nature of the church."* [12] There has been a latent conflict in Protestantism which has been gathering momentum for more than half a century. In some sense, the sources of the conflict go back to the origins of Protestantism. Hadden mentions three major sources of conflict: lack of understanding (1) the church, (2) faith, and (3) authority. The clergy have worked out a new understanding of the purpose and meaning of the church, but did not communicate the new view to the laity. The same is true of the content of the faith. As a result there is a clash between clergy and laity, a struggle over authority. While for a long, long time pastors have run the churches as they have seen fit, now laity are questioning the basic presuppositions of their authority.

Thus far much of the laity understood the church as comforter. But the new type of minister sees the church more as challenger amid social strife: "As the New Breed pushes for greater commitment to the challenger role, growing evidence suggests that there is an inherent conflict between the roles of comforter and challenger." [13] Only a few laymen are joining the new ministers in their zeal for social justice. So a growing number of clergy supported by a few laymen are pitted against a block of conservative clergy and a large majority of laymen. [14]

The conflict comes to a head especially in matters of belief. It is quite obvious that a change has taken place in the faith of the church. But thus far hardly anyone has gotten a feel for the total picture. What one notices is the shift of emphasis: *"The Christian religion, for an increasing number of clergy, is a faith professing a heritage which instructs men in the meaning of life rather than a dogmatic tradition proclaiming to possess ultimate reality."* [15] As a consequence there is no common agreement as to what

[11] Jeffrey K. Hadden, *The Gathering Storm in the Churches* (Garden City, 1969), p. 3.
[12] *Ibid.*, p. 5.
[13] *Ibid.*, p. 6.
[14] *Ibid.*, p. 15.
[15] *Ibid.*, p. 61.

must be believed and what is central and peripheral, *"nor is there any clear authority to resolve the uncertainty."* [16]

Here we are zeroing in on the crucial issue. While many claims have been made by churchmen as regards the need for social justice and a new meaning of life, seldom is it understood that all this is not immediately evident as Christian affirmation. Too little has there been a common mind in Protestantism on the basis of these claims. Everyman has been able to become his own judge. Hadden comes close to stating the problem. But, because of the sociological character of the analysis, it remains largely descriptive: "The question of authority looms very large. As a doctrine of infallible truth, Christianity possesses an enormous authority. It is a belief system which professes to hold the essence of truth about the nature and meaning of life, a system which offers rewards for those who believe and practice this doctrine of truth and punishes those who reject it. But when the foundations of this belief system are no longer certain, what happens to authority?" [17] The descriptive assessment of the situation has to be supplemented by a critical theological assessment. It is insufficient to point out that the clergy as a group by and large are *for* the achievement of social justice. What many do not realize is that in all their striving for justice they still may not be getting at the real dilemmas of the church. They are uneasy because they feel that something is wrong. And so they move from the church as comforter to the church as challenger. But do they grasp the inadequacy of the overall framework in which this transition takes place? Few really tackle the basic problem that underlies the uncertainty and confusion. Claims for social justice are often made because right now it is the thing to do. At the same time the foundations for any Christian claim are rejected or made light of.

The New Relativism in American Theology

Much of the blame for the uneasy situation in the church must be laid at the doorsteps of theology. The theology that gains the attention of the American public by and large has given up any hard-nosed commitment in establishing a real point of common reference to which one could appeal in good conscience. The surrender that is taking place is described with exceptional clarity in Michael Novak's essay on "The New Relativism in American Theology." [18] One of the major reasons for the decline of authority is the waning denominationalism in this country: "Confidence in the rightness and adequacy of limited traditions has been shaken by the

[16] *Ibid.,* p. 66.
[17] *Ibid.*
[18] Michael Novak, "The New Relativism in American Theology," in Donald R. Cutler, ed., *The Religious Situation: 1968* (Boston, 1968), pp. 197 ff.

discovery of the power of other traditions. Whereas churches and denominations used to boast of their own advantages, now they are recognizing the advantages of others. . . . A great many supposed theological differences appear, in this new light, to have been based on sociological differences." [19] So what one discovers is the richness of human beliefs and the relativity of human values. It is significant how Novak handles this in terms of principle: "It is true that men differ and that each man must define his own horizon; it does not follow that one horizon is as adequate as another, but only that there is no way of appealing to some umpire outside the playing field." [20]

The notion that there might be an umpire outside the separate playing fields should not be so readily discarded. There are some questions that cannot be decided without a common umpire. For example, the question of who man is to be. Here we have a thickening of the plot. Time and again Novak appeals to the *actual* relativism of the American experience. He lifts it out with considerable pride, as it were: "The experience of living in American society provides a lived relativism. No one view of life, no one set of values, can be taken for granted. The conclusion to be drawn is not that one view is as good as another; it is that each view must prove itself under the critical eye of others." [21] But here ultimately man himself, with his uncertainty of himself, becomes the measure of truth. Radical theology especially contributes to making this direction dominant. And Novak supports the trend. He sees that the radical movement repeats "to an amazing degree, in form if not in content, Feuerbach's program of reducing theology to anthropology." [22] And Novak would somehow wish to move even more radically in this direction focusing on what human beings may ascertain of themselves: "In countless records of contemporary experience, unreflected upon, unthematized, and unpenetrated, there lie testimonials to the perennial power of the human being to marvel at his own identity, to question it, and to delight in its elusiveness." [23] This emphasis on man offers the possibility for the American theologian to interpret the reality of God in completely immanental, secular, and historical terms.[24] There may be many who have a high sense of appreciation for what Christianity stands for and contributes. But they do not feel the need to identify with Christianity and make it their own: "Thus it happens that many who understand full well the *empirical* meaning of the wisdom of the Christian faith and realize it in their lives—love of God, love of neighbor, purity of heart, courage unto death—do not, nevertheless, interpret the meaning of

[19] *Ibid.*, p. 201.
[20] *Ibid.*, p. 202.
[21] *Ibid.*, p. 210.
[22] *Ibid.*, p. 211.
[23] *Ibid.*, p. 214.
[24] *Ibid.*, p. 217.

their lives through that name which for Christians is above all names, the name of Jesus." [25]

Novak singles out Bonhoeffer as one who made too much of a good thing by stressing the need human beings have for Jesus and the church. He agrees with Bonhoeffer that the church may have some significance as a community of power and grace. But he regards Bonhoeffer's view as much too narrow and makes every effort to move beyond him: "More extensively than he, one might also see many other communities not only of power and grace, but also of revelation, accurate interpretation, and illuminating symbols of the same word." [26] If Novak's description of American theology is accurate and if his position represents the logical outcome of the general trend, the result is a sheer negation of Christian authority in any sense. An acceptance of relativism leads ultimately to sheer predilection of whim and fancy. Nothing can be negotiated in terms of what is ultimately true. What counts is what pleases.

The Liberating Word as Authority

The fact that the Word of God can no longer function as an arbiter of truth is becoming more and more the bane of the church. Since no umpire is acknowledged who could arbitrate between the various games being played, we readily put ourselves in his place. From our perspective it is the unwillingness of American theology to root itself in the biblical word that lies at the root of the lack of any true authority. Langdon Gilkey has recently argued the reasons for this unwillingness in a principal way. His first step is to eliminate the primal significance of the Word for faith by declaring that it is no longer acknowledged as present: "One cannot begin . . . with the presupposition of the presence of the Word of God, if one is asking the question of God. . . . If the question of *God* is raised, theology literally must begin from the beginning, it must deal with its own most basic foundations. . . . [It] means starting as best one can on one's own and at the level of concrete experience." [27] Here right away we get caught in a nest of difficulties: "Theology literally must begin . . . with its own most basic foundations." Who decides what these most basic foundations are? Gilkey? The philosophy of religion? Philosophical theology? Or what? Here immediately we are facing a *real* plight. All too quickly a category

[25] *Ibid.*, p. 223.

[26] *Ibid.*

[27] Langdon Gilkey, *Naming the Whirlwind: The Renewal of God-Language* (Indianapolis and New York, 1969), p. 11. It is almost awkward that one feels constrained to raise radically critical questions of such an achievement of scholarly integrity as Gilkey's book. But part of the awkward aspect of the matter is that some of the issues appear not even to be *seen* as issues. How does one communicate theologically in such a situation?

mistake can slip into the argument and we become implicated in a philosophy of religion as the most basic foundation of theology rather than the church or the covenant community. While we certainly can no longer operate with the idea that everyone in Western civilization will acknowledge God, in the covenant community we can still begin with a Word-presence that seeks to point to God. There is no other function of theology.

Of course, Gilkey feels that we can no longer speak effectively of a church community that believes in God. But that means that the weight of the argument rests merely with the doubters and the talkers. Gilkey believes "that the Church is permeated by the world's spirit, and thus no useful distinction for the purposes of theological method can be made between a theological starting point relevant for the Church and one relevant for the world." [28] That the church is permeated by the world's spirit is no reason to equivocate on the presence of the remnant in the church. Gilkey does not hit upon the idea that there may be a battle in the church between the false church and the remnant. And so he rejects the idea completely that the church may be a valid starting point for theology: "The actual Church is one of doubt and secularity as well as of halting faith. No wonder a theology which assumes that all of its hearers have experienced the reality of God through the hearing of the Word, and goes on from there, seems often unreal." [29] But the whole point of some "church" theologies, or better church-oriented theologies, is that not all of its hearers have experienced the reality of God through the hearing of the Word. It is exactly this hearing of the Word which cannot be presupposed and which makes theology necessary. What must be presupposed is the presence of the Word—otherwise there would be no church left. In other words, it is not the faithfulness or the faithlessness of the church which needs to be appealed to as the foundation of the church, but the faithfulness of the Word. What does this strange phenomenon, the Word, mean? What does it mean that the church is *given* the Book?

Why does not Gilkey think of raising the question of what this gift does to the church? In keeping with his argument he says about those who wish to take the church as starting point of theology seriously: "The theological error involved here . . . is the effort to base an *actual* theology on the *invisible* Church, to found theological language not on what is actual about people and their experience, but on what is itself an article of belief." [30] But doesn't Gilkey make a category mistake here? He suggests that theology is beginning with an invisible church, if it begins with the Word itself. But the whole point is that theology, because of the usual unfaithfulness of the church (something which Gilkey rightly sees), must begin with

[28] *Ibid.*, pp. 22-23.
[29] *Ibid.*, p. 195.
[30] *Ibid.*, p. 196.

the Word itself. It is the Word of the Book which determines the theological task. It communicates a reality claim that theology must explicate with reference to reality, albeit from within the context of the church.

The biblical word is battling against the threat to humanity. Jesus Christ presented a truth about what it means to be a man. This truth has been questioned time and again. It is also questioned today. The whole point as to there being no umpire (Novak) gets a different slant from here. Arbitrarily no one can decide whether there is an umpire or not. There simply *is* an umpire if the Word proves itself as such in its presence. In the battle against inhumanity the Word evidences itself. If any man wills to do this Word he will know whether it is true. The truth about man is not something that is already defined in an eternal structure. It is always created in the encounter with the Word, as new possibilities for humanization are opened up by the Word itself.

The other side of this experience is the fact of man's unfreedom. The major theological question today is to what extent man is free at all to think what he ought and to do what he ought. As long as men today believe that man somehow is able to grasp the "ultimate ought" under which he stands and to realize it, the question of the Word of God will be treated with little seriousness. Only a sense of man's captivity will make theology turn to the Word as the liberating Word. And theology will realize that only with respect to man's captivity does the real problem of authority emerge.

The Question of Heresy Revisited

That there is conflict in the American church has probably been amply documented in this essay. But in trying to describe the features of the struggle over the authority of the Word of God, we have not as yet pointed to the most radical dimension of the conflict. What is at stake is ultimately the question of heresy—a false teaching. We are initially thinking here of heresy the way Karl Rahner has defined it: "Heresy is always a doctrine which, contrary to intention, threatens the whole of one's spiritual existence, insofar as this existence is based on the reference to the one complete event of revelation which even the heretic affirms." [31] In our situation today it is a question of a false teaching about the nature of man.

Lest the conflict we are involved in be misunderstood completely, we must stress that it is not so much a conflict with flesh and blood, but with powers and principalities. As regards the conflict between Russia and America, it was recently observed: "It would be helpful for everyone to demythologize his thinking instead of nourishing absolute images of good

[31] Karl Rahner, *Theological Investigations*, V (Baltimore, 1966), 470.

and bad guys." [32] This also pertains very much to the conflict in the church. The time of heresy-hunting is past. In many instances, individuals are singularly no longer so significant that they could be made exclusively responsible for the course of events. Ideologies and structures are now the real villains. The new heresies are compounds of generations of misapprehensions about the nature of man and his relationship to his environment.

Systems have developed that have institutionalized these misapprehensions and created entirely new structures beyond the control of any single individual. In regard to capitalism it was recently said: "The profiteering could be eliminated; the technocracy would remain in force." [33] So we today cannot speak of heresy so much with respect to the individual, but more in reference to those powers that today, unless brought under control, are capable of destroying man. It is here that the question of heresy becomes the question of the political and public truth about man. We need to understand what true manhood is. And we need to condemn falsehood about man, just as many dwellings today need to be condemned because they create inhuman living conditions.

While all the facets of the present authority problem we have pointed to are significant relative to the question of heresy, the issue of *racism* is perhaps the place where contemporary American man's self-contradiction becomes most tangible and pressing. For in racism collective man rationalizes and secures his power over the neighbor. When the purpose of life has largely become the accumulation of wealth, the exploitation of the neighbor is almost an inevitable consequence. Today the pursuit of wealth for its own sake is largely taken for granted as a good thing. But it was only "by the end of the fifteenth century . . . that the pursuit of wealth for its own sake became the chief motive of human activity." [34] I do not wish to bemoan things that can no longer be changed. But it must be realized quite clearly that in the process of pursuing wealth for its own sake man lost sight of the dignity of the neighbor, making him a thing. This is what lies at the root of the evil of racism: "The Negro was a thing to be used, not a person to be respected." [35]

If it were possible to stop viewing man as a thing in one context of American life today, this might be a first step of conquering the heresy about man also in other areas. But the whole problem is not as yet viewed in its radical depth. The premise is usually that man, without the influence of the liberating Word, is capable of viewing the neighbor as more than a thing. This is exactly, in an ultimate sense, what the Word denies. That is,

[32] *Time* (November 7, 1969), p. 18.

[33] Theodore Roszak, *The Making of a Counter Culture* (Garden City, 1969), p. 19.

[34] Harold J. Laski, *The Rise of Liberalism: The Philosophy of a Business Civilization* (New York and London, 1936), p. 12.

[35] Martin Luther King, Jr., *Where Do We Go from Here: Chaos or Community?* (Boston, 1968), p. 39.

the Word denies that man can really be free without God's intervention in Jesus Christ.

Since this is the case, nothing is gained for finding a solution, for example, by appealing to a "black theology which rejects Pauline theology and claims that Jesus was the liberator of the oppressed." [36] In trying to come to grips with the new heresies, we need to get away from misconceptions of the nature of the biblical word. If we grasp that Jesus indeed is the liberator and liberation is always mediated through him, we might be able to view the apostle Paul as an early interpreter of this liberation, albeit under circumstances quite different from our present conditions of oppression. There is no reason whatsoever to play off Jesus as liberator from oppression against Paul as an early interpreter of Christian liberation or vice versa. The question is in what sense early Christian experiences of liberation were authorized —brought into being—by the liberation accomplished by Jesus of Nazareth. The entire biblical witness needs to be examined as to what extent this liberation rejects a particular view of man and introduces a new view. The new view of man is what the present conflict in the church is all about.

"The most dangerous moment comes when all values are in flux. The Seventies confront us with such a moment. For guidance, we look not out into space but back from space toward our own Planet." [37] Wherever we turn, there is conflict over values today.[38] For the church, the basic dimension of the conflict is over the value of freedom. Finally the question is as to what extent man can be free both privately and publicly. The black today is the model of human longing for freedom in both respects. He knows that so long as he is not free politically he is also not free spiritually. Insofar as the new heresies are concerned, it is becoming clearer every day that the basic attempt to create freedom will not succeed unless man is liberated for freedom in both respects. Freedom is not an accomplishment of man, but a gift. Man, however, no longer senses this. And so he determines his freedom in whatever way he sees fit. The exploitation of the fellowman is one of its consequences. The false understanding of the nature of man in modern society will be overcome only by a new understanding of freedom as grounded in the liberating Word.

Technically the mandate of liberation must be discussed in the context of how the methodological issues are argued in theology right now. Focusing on theological ethics, Gibson Winter has pinpointed the context with great clarity: "Theological ethics is a creative work of discerning the meanings within effective structures in the light of meanings disclosed in biblical

---

[36] Quoted in *News on Christian Unity*, 9:10 (December 10, 1969), p. 3.

[37] George B. Leonard, "A Place for Snakes as well as Naked Lovers," *Look,* 34:1 (January 13, 1970), p. 81.

[38] Cf. John J. Corson, "Social Change and the University," *Saturday Review* (January 10, 1970), p. 78.

events. . . . Karl Mannheim referred to such events as *paradigmatic events,* which convey in the form of action those meanings which shape and direct life. . . . Paradigmatic events have to be translated into contemporary patterns which embody their essential meaning. . . . The paradigmatic events give gestalts of meaning as they are appropriated in faith, but those meanings are also constituted by the historical consciousness which apprehends them. . . . The ultimacy disclosed in a paradigmatic event is not diminished by the relativity of our appropriation, but our appropriation is not to be confused with that ultimacy." [39] This is an utterly clear description of what is at stake in principle. But Winter in speaking of ultimacy has left out the most basic dimension of the Christian paradigmatic event, which is the origination of liberation. For without this origination there could be no human freedom. Theology cannot skip over this dimension of the origination of Christian thought and action. For it is this origination that overcomes man's inability to translate the paradigmatic event into present-day life. Only as the liberating Word mediates the liberation accomplished in Jesus Christ is the conflict of the church redirected into new creative experiences of freedom.

In the new church conflict we are compelled to move from the church as comforter, not to the church as challenger, but to the church as liberator, on grounds of the liberating Word that today makes efficacious the liberation accomplished by Jesus Christ.

A Transatlantic Merging of the Conflict?

The essays presented in this volume obviously reflect the concerns of theologians on the other side of the Atlantic. And yet their concerns in several ways cover themes pervading the American scene. The German situation, because of its recent history, has a natural affinity to the contemporary American church conflict. The reintroduction into the American theological debate of the concept of heresy by James H. Cone[40] echoes the European debate of almost fourty years ago.[41] Interestingly enough, the first reference to an American church conflict (*Kirchenkampf*) that came to my attention was in a European publication.[42]

[39] Gibson Winter, "Theology and Social Science," in Daniel T. Jenkins, ed., *The Scope of Theology* (Cleveland and New York, 1965), pp. 193-95.

[40] James H. Cone, *Black Theology and Black Power,* p. 103. It is one of the merits of Cone's book to have sharply delineated where the crucial issue of the debate is to be found.

[41] See Arthur C. Cochrane, *The Church's Confession Under Hitler* (Philadelphia, 1962).

[42] Heinrich Hellstern, *Mississippi* (Basel, 1969), p. 68. In the United States for a goodly while the issue was discussed under the heading of the "Underground Church." See Malcolm Boyd, ed., *The Underground Church* (New York, 1968).—It was only after the manuscript for this book had gone to the printer that John C. Bennett's sermon, "The Great Controversy in the Churches," appeared; *The Christian Century,* 87:21 (May 27, 1970), pp. 659-

The essays center around the nature of the Word of God. For a while, a discussion on this matter may have seemed only a remote need on the American continent. But no longer so.[43] Significantly these essays either directly by quotation, or at least indirectly in terms of general sensibility, refer to the American debate—as the reader will discover for himself. It remains for us merely to point to the core of the argument. Eberhard Jüngel introduces the positive affirmation: "Whoever, without justification, continues to talk about God in avoidance of the Word of God, talks God to death. And whoever, avoiding the Word of God, forgoes talk about God, silences God to death. In order that God be neither talked to death nor silenced to death, the Word of God demands undivided linguistic attention." This kind of emphasis, however, is by no means uniformly accepted. Especially practical theology has questioned the continued emphasis on the Word. A spokesman of the opposition has been Hans-Dieter Bastian: "*Either* practical theology follows the doctrine of the Word and gains certainty dogmatically, but loses reality practically, *or* it turns away from the axiomatic Word to human words, accepts the responsibility for their power and powerlessness and subjects the church's speaking and acting to radical empirical analysis. This second way . . . we would like to commend."

That one can get along better with "less Word" and "more words" is, however, doubted, especially among some exegetes. Hans Conzelmann once more calls attention to the Word of God and emphasizes its significance in Christian communication: "Proclamation should not seek points of contact in feelings of sinfulness, cosmic threats, or other anxieties. Instead, its task is to make contact on grounds of the capacity of the Word." Hans-Joachim Kraus for the Old Testament perspective points very much to the same mandate: "Must not a new listening to the Old Testament explode the anthropological *incurvatio in hominem?*" With this question in mind he immediately meets the death-of-God issue head on.

In the present theological situation in America there is still a great reluctance to take the Word of Scripture seriously. We are offering these essays for American reflection in the hope that the radical issues of the present debate are grasped more fully as reaching from continent to continent. The appeal to the Word does not imply submission to a straitjacket of ancient ideas. The Word is simply that creative force which evokes the possibilities of new life.[44] The debate imposes upon us a common challenge lest we forget that Word "above all earthly powers."

---

63. It is "must" reading for anyone who wants to understand the far-reaching dimensions of the present church conflict. A valuable contribution to this whole issue is also Leander E. Keck and James E. Sellers, "Theological Ethics in an American Crisis," *Interpretation*, 24:4 (October, 1970), pp. 456-81.

[43] Cf. James D. Smart, *The Divided Mind of Modern Theology* (Philadelphia, 1967), pp. 13 ff.

[44] Cf. my essay, "Theology of Liberation," *Continuum*, 7:4 (Winter, 1970), pp. 520 ff.

I

GOD—AS A WORD OF OUR LANGUAGE*

For Helmut Gollwitzer on His Sixtieth Birthday

EBERHARD JÜNGEL

Who is God that we *must* speak of him? Is "God" still a word in our language that we *can* speak of him?

I

The problem of our talk about God today arises in the dialectic between these two questions. For today, in this dialectic, the ever essential dialogue of Christian faith with the language of the world takes place. Without dialogue with the language of the world Christian faith would simply not come to speech at all. In fact, in every period of its history Christian faith must necessarily find its language in the language of the world.

But precisely herein faith today is confronted with particular difficulties. Our language no longer tends naturally toward talk about God. It rather resists everything that relates to our world in a non-worldly way and that appears to bring the world into question. The matter-of-course fashion in which earlier times came to speak of God strikes us as distant and alien.

In *The Arabian Nights* we are told of a lover who is about to free his

* This expanded draft of my inaugural lecture at the University of Zürich was also the basis of various lectures delivered at a number of German and foreign universities. Translated by Robert T. Osborn, Duke University, from *Evangelische Theologie*, 29:1 (January, 1969), pp. 1-24.

beloved from an evil demon that has abducted her: "Then a drowsiness overcame him, and he fell asleep—glorious is He who never sleeps." Hugo von Hofmannsthal found in these lines the particular and incomparable charm of oriental language and poetry: "Thus to let the feeling of God emerge from nothingness into a chaotic adventure, like the moon when it appears beyond the perimeter of the horizon." [1] And yet, the *past* of our Western language is infinitely closer to the Eastern matter-of-course way, in which the sleeping lover becomes the occasion for praise of him "who never sleeps," than to our *contemporary* language. In *The Arabian Nights* there lurks "a presentiment, a presence of God in all these sensual matters, which is indescribable." [2] In the Christian linguistic tradition one finds presentiment of God in all that is non-sensual or trans-sensual, an intuition which found an even more precise expression on account of the experience of the hiddenness of God. Today there is nothing comparable. Our language gives us no presentiment either of God's presence or his absence. It is without religious sensibility. Its limits refer us back to the world, not beyond it.

The language of our world has become more worldly. The holy must let itself be perceived profanely if it is at all to be able to sanctify. Living in our time has become more temporal. And the eternal must occur temporally if it is to open up eternal life at all. That the holy *can* express itself profanely, that the eternal *can* become temporal—this is an ancient experience. But that it *must* do this, that the holy can be thought of as healing *only* within the order of the profane and not otherwise, and that the eternal can be understood as eternal *only* as a historical event and not otherwise—this is our experience and our problem.

Before we direct ourselves more closely to this problem, we should nevertheless be warned not to see in this event—designated today, as a rule, as the process of total secularization—a disaster. Secularization is anything but "a theologically conditioned bad category" (*eine theologisch bedingte Unrechtskategorie*), anything but the epitome of that "which, 'as regards the substance,' should not be." [3] Much rather, it may be shown[4] that "secularization" is itself largely a consequence of the dialogue of Christian faith with the language of the world or something like a worldly consequence of the Word of God. And the unprecedented difficulties that today attend the inescapable attempt of Christian faith to talk about God are perhaps at the same time the unprecedented opportunities of faith to come closer linguistically to its subject matter than was possible within a metaphysically formed linguistic tradition.

[1] *1001 Nacht* ([*The Arabian Nights*] Leipzig, n.d.) I, 13.

[2] *Ibid.*, p. 12.

[3] H. Blumenberg, *Die Legitimität der Neuzeit* (Frankfurt, 1966), p. 73, with a quote from C. H. Ratschow, "Säkularismus," in R.G.G. (3rd ed.), V, 1288.

[4] Friedrich Gogarten has, in his own way, demonstrated this point.

Certainly unprecedented difficulties do exist. They must be recognized as such if faith is not to terminate in a (certainly only all too eloquent) speechlessness. Christian faith today is threatened by speechlessness—not because words fail it, but because the right words fail it. The speechlessness threatening Christian faith is at the same time an elementary threat to the subject matter of the Christian faith. For the subject matter of Christian faith compellingly seeks to come to speech. If the right words remain wanting, then the one who thinks he understands is obviously not as yet grasped by the subject matter. Therefore we began reflecting on the problem of contemporary talk about God with the dialectic of two inseparable questions, one concerning the subject matter and the other concerning the language:

Who is God that we *must* speak of him?

Is "God" still a word in our language that we *can* speak of him?

II

Let us turn first to the second question. A consultation of the dictionary will quickly convince us that the word "God" still appears in our language. Of course, anyone today who seeks an answer to our question in the dictionary is probably not seriously asking whether the word "God" still appears in our language. There is no question at all that it does, although this language of ours is different from that of our forefathers. For them the Bible was still their "linguistic home," and "God was more or less their linguistic center." [5] The language we speak is acquainted with "God" as a word that, while it is known to everybody, nevertheless seems no longer appropriate to that language. It no longer speaks. "God," as a word in our language, has as such no longer anything to say. It still functions in a few polite forms of speech, in a certain matter-of-course way. "For God's sake"; "Oh, my God"; "By God." Such expressions as these still come to our lips automatically. We can still chatter about God—in the communist East as well as in the capitalist West. And when theologians speak of God? Then the word "God" is, as it were, *methodologically* installed in its language function. But it obviously does not naturally appear as other words usually do when we speak.

Gerhard Ebeling recognized in this situation the danger that "we threaten to die of language poisoning. This is not because God has completely died from our language, but because God is festering in our language." [6] And he insists that "we must not irresponsibly continue to talk of God, nor irresponsibly stop doing so." [7] With this postulate Ebeling has formulated what our speech demands of us with reference to the word "God." What

[5] G. Ebeling, *Gott und Wort* (Tübingen, 1966), p. 13.
[6] *Ibid.*, p. 11.
[7] *Ibid.*, p. 13.

is my duty where words are concerned? This is Ebeling's leading question.[8]

This question about my responsibility for the word "God" relates to the question of my responsibility for word as such, but not as a special case to a general one. Rather, according to Ebeling, "reflection on the meaning of the nature of word" in general leads to "an understanding of what 'God' signifies." [9] This means, admittedly, that in the experience of our responsibility for the word we can experience what the word "God" has to say. Whoever wants to say what "God" means must, according to Ebeling, point to "an area of universal human experience," because only therein is "the meaning of the word 'God' verifiable." [10] According to Ebeling, it is within the horizon of our obligation to language that the word "God" can be verified.

However we do not owe language this or that or any other *thing*. Rather, we owe language *ourselves*. Man is required to speak, and thereby he shows that he is obligated to language. Precisely herein is he man. Accordingly, Ebeling designates the "basic situation of man" as "word situation." To this word situation the word "God" refers; indeed, "the word 'God' means the basic situation of man as word situation," so that "by speaking of God man is made accountable for his linguisticality. . . . And indeed the word 'God' shows us that man in his linguisticality is not master of himself. . . . No one can speak independently." This fact, that man "in his linguisticality essentially is not self-sufficient," must, according to Ebeling, be interpreted from the standpoint of his co-humanity, although it cannot be understood completely from this perspective. Rather, it is here that the word "God" indicates the fact that "in every word event there is present a 'depth dimension' to which every word owes its existence. . . . 'God'—that is the mystery of reality [that] addresses man as to the situation that lets him be a recipient only, tolerates no neutrality, and expects from man a responsible account of all that concerns him." As the mystery of reality the word "God" is a demand—the demand for a very definite movement, the movement that directs man into the situation "in which the genuine use of the word 'God' is that of the vocative, of address." [11]

Ebeling's attempt to locate a meaningful place for the word "God" in the context of words (namely, the place that, as the basic situation of man, alone makes possible the event of language and thus the context of words in general) represents a kind of hermeneutical verification of the word "God." Surprising in this hermeneutical verification (within a general horizon of experience) is the notion that the word "God" can be conceived as functioning independently of the proclamation of the gospel. To be sure,

[8] *Ibid.*, p. 18.
[9] *Ibid.*
[10] *Ibid.*, p. 54.
[11] *Ibid.*, pp. 54-63.

man needs this proclamation, according to Ebeling, so that "the movement thus required of man by the word 'God' " may reach its goal (the calling upon God). But it is the directed movement toward the goal, that man is being assigned the situation of prayer, which is the verifiable meaning of the word "God," independent of the proclamation of the gospel. Borrowing a Reformation distinction, we might say that the hermeneutical verification of the word "God" does not occur in the horizon of the gospel, but rather in the horizon of "my obligation to the word," that is, in the horizon of the law, so that the event of the speaking about God may be truly a matter of gospel.

So fruitful a theological approach invites discussion. One of the aims of the following reflections is to contribute to a discussion. Points of contact and differences will be intertwined. This becomes clear already in the question about the being of God (the question which precedes that about the use of the word "God"), namely, who is God that we *must* speak of him?

This question proceeds from the assumption that the word "God" does not determine its function in our language, that it does not indicate the use we are to make of it. Who God is is not revealed by the word "God." Only God himself declares who God is. But God discloses who he is when he necessitates our speech about him, and with this necessity authorizes us to make use of the word "God." This means, in the first place, that the significance of the word "God" is decided not only by its use, but by the necessity of its use. Where the word "God" is not necessary it is superfluous. It must, however, be God himself who makes the word "God" and talk about God necessary—or else the word remains superfluous.[12] This is my presupposition when I contend that the question of whether God is still a word in our language can be discussed meaningfully only when it is raised together with the other question of who God is that we must speak of him.

Of course, this presupposition is not one that arises by itself out of our contemporary speech. It is also anything but the attempt to impose a presupposition upon our language; for this presupposition implies exactly the thesis that the necessary use of the word "God" can arise only *as our talk* about God. God is, if he himself makes speech necessary, never a speech premise but, rather, always a concrete speech event. God introduces himself by speaking. Every *verbum dei est dei loquentis persona.*

Thus the necessity to speak of God is grounded in the fact that God brings his being into appearance as word, that in speaking he introduces himself. Indeed, even this sentence is already the result of the occurrence of an event of human speech which at least once happened concretely, namely,

[12] Rudolf Bultmann probably meant precisely this when he answered the question: What meaning does it have to speak of God? by saying that "the decision (as to whether we should speak of God or keep silent) is God's. . . . And in fact, the only answer to the question—if and when we can speak of God—is: when we *must.*" *Glauben und Verstehen,* I (Tübingen, 1961), 34 .

confession of Jesus Christ as the man in whom God has brought his being into appearance as word. Accordingly, the Gospel of John, speaking of Jesus, confesses that in the beginning was the Word, and the Word was with God, and the Word was God. The fact that these pronouncements about God and Word pertain to Jesus Christ discloses the uniqueness that is appropriate to this man with regard to our talk about God. Christology is theology κατ' ἐξοχήν. If anywhere at all, then it is in Christology that the use of the word "God" proves its necessity.

III

If we are to understand who Jesus Christ is, then *God* must come to speech. At the same time, conversely, the way in which God *must* come to speech, if we are to understand Jesus as the Christ, primarily determines who God is. If, when we do not talk about God, we do not understand who Jesus Christ is, then we do comprehend who God is only when we speak of him in connection with Jesus Christ. Thus the being of Jesus Christ both makes talk about God necessary and makes such talk unequivocal. That is, talk about God becomes clear through the very fact that it is unconditionally necessary for the understanding of the being of Jesus Christ. Everything that is and has become permits, if need be, of being understood without talk about God. Theologians of the early church expressed this fact with extreme precision when they designated confession of Jesus Christ as ἡ περὶ σωτῆρος θεολογία or as ἡ τοῦ υἱοῦ θεολογία.

Today, however, this issue—the question of who Jesus Christ is—is a matter of disagreement. It has experienced its sharpest expression of late in the fact that it is no longer under discussion *how* one must speak of God in order to understand who Jesus is, but rather *if* for this purpose one must speak of God at all. In America, and now also in Germany, a death-of-God theology has arisen, whose various representatives are agreed in the opinion that human language in our secular age is not able to stake out a meaningful place for the word "God." In entering this debate we limit ourselves here to a discussion of a particular contention of the death-of-God theology, namely, the thesis of language analysis that the use of the word "God" within the limits of our language is not verifiable.

This thesis is represented "theologically" by Paul M. van Buren, who thinks he must speak of God *in the language of the world* in such a way that one no longer speaks of *God* at all. Van Buren understands his consequent undertaking as Christology. He intends to make his Barthian heritage agree with the neopositive language philosophy by avoiding, in the context of talk about Jesus Christ, any talk about God altogether, and thus also any natural theology. This certainly creates the impression that here the devil has been driven out by Beelzebub. But let us take a closer look.

Van Buren understands his approach as a language analysis of the gospel, guided by the methodological insight that all linguistic statements must be verifiable empirically. Now the language of the gospel cannot be reduced simply to such statements. Biblical talk about the acts of God, for instance, is meaningless if it is understood as a direct empirical declaration about the world, because "theological statements . . . are meaningless in a secular age when they are taken as straightforward empirical assertions about the world." [13] The theological assertions of biblical language are meaningful, then, in our empirical age only when one succeeds in showing that they are the kinds of assertions that "have a use and a meaning as the expressions of a historical perspective with far-reaching empirical consequences in a man's life."

In this fashion van Buren interprets biblical and ecclesiastical talk about Jesus as a construction of faith pronouncements *"which express, describe, or commend a particular way of seeing the world, other men, and oneself, and the way of life appropriate to such a perspective. . . . The norm of the Christian perspective is the series of events to which the New Testament documents testify, centering in the life, death, and resurrection of Jesus of Nazareth."* In order in an empirical world to give currency to the meaning of the words which the New Testament used in the context of these events, one must find appropriate and clear expressions that measure up to the aforementioned verification principle. However, this means, for example, that in talking about the raising of Jesus from the dead, talk about God as the one who raised him must be excluded. The resurrection of Jesus means, according to van Buren, the following: "Jesus of Nazareth was a free man in his own life, who attracted followers and created enemies according to the dynamics of personality and in a manner comparable to the effect of other liberated persons in history upon people about them. He died as a result of the threat that such a free man poses for insecure and bound men. His disciples were left no less insecure and frightened. Two days later, Peter, and then other disciples, had an experience of which Jesus was the sense-content. They experienced a discernment situation in which Jesus the free man whom they had known, themselves, and indeed the whole world, were seen in a quite new way. From that moment, the disciples began to possess something of the freedom of Jesus. His freedom began to be 'contagious.' For the disciples, therefore, the story of Jesus could not be told simply as the story of a free man who had died. Because of the new way in which the disciples saw him and because of what had happened to them, the story had to include the event of Easter. In telling the story of Jesus of Nazareth, therefore, they told it as the story of the free man who had set them free. This was the story which they proclaimed as the Gospel for all men." [14]

[13] Paul van Buren, *The Secular Meaning of the Gospel* (New York, 1963), p. 199.
[14] *Ibid.*, p. 134.

31

Van Buren commends this interpretation of the language of New Testament Christology as a contemporary exegesis that "provides a logical account of the language of Christian faith without resort to a misleading use of words." [15]

To such misleading use of words belongs, according to van Buren, also the continuing use of biblical God talk. Therefore he recommends that the use of the word "God" be avoided, "because it equivocates and misleads. It seems to be a proper name, calling up the image of a divine entity, but it refuses to function as any other proper name does." Therefore, the "interpretation of the language of the Gospel which does not necessitate assertions concerning 'the nature and activities of a supposed personal creator'" is obligatory. Van Buren radically demands a "discarding [of] some of the traditional language of Christianity, no matter how much other ages have revered this language." The discarded terms will be, basically, merely "cherished traditions." It would appear, then, that biblical and church talk about God belong to the same category.

Van Buren demands of theology "the sort of reduction which has been made by modern culture in many fields. Astrology has been 'reduced' to astronomy, for example. . . . Alchemy was 'reduced' to chemistry by the rigorous application of an empirical method. . . . In almost every field of human learning, the metaphysical and cosmological aspect has disappeared and the subject matter has been 'limited' to the human, the historical, the empirical. Theology cannot escape this tendency if it is to be a serious mode of contemporary thought, and such a 'reduction' of content need no more be regretted in theology than in astronomy, chemistry, or painting." [16] What one can say about Jesus verifies itself in the description of the process that is kindled by the gospel in its hearer: "The light will dawn; he will be possessed of a new way of seeing himself, the world, and all things, and he will 'catch' something of the contagious freedom of Jesus." He will be possessed of a new way of seeing all things, *but not of seeing God.* That God made this Jesus—who knew no sin—sin for us (II Cor. 5:21) now means that "he [Jesus] 'put himself in their shoes'; he carried their burdens," and his death is the consequence of this life. Of course van Buren talks about Jesus as the one who "died for me, for my forgiveness and freedom." [17] But precisely in view of such a contention the question about the subject who forgives becomes imperative and inescapable. Who forgives sin if not God?

IV

Our counterquestion was until now provoked by the thrust of van Buren's argument. Yet we must raise a question about the problem as defined by

[15] *Ibid.*, p. 145.
[16] *Ibid.*, p. 198.
[17] *Ibid.*, pp. 151-53.

van Buren in a way that comes to grips with the definition of the problem itself.

Against van Buren's argument that the word "God" is ambiguous and misleading, theology has nothing to say. That word is, in fact, more than ambiguous, which was of course already clear to the biblical writers. The Old Testament conflict between God and the idols has to do *de facto* with the effort to let the equivocal word "God" become unequivocal through its proper use. "I am the Lord your God; you shall have no other gods before me." The first of all the commandments has axiomatic force for all talk about God. Even our talk about Jesus Christ can be understood only as an interpretation of this commandment. Accordingly, New Testament faith in Jesus Christ polemicizes against the φύσει μὴ ὄντες θεοί (Gal. 4:8). Can one speak of Jesus Christ without at the same time involving the relevance of the distinction between God and the idols? Does not the forgoing of talk about God mean, as a matter of fact, the identification of God and the idols? Who would God be that we should be allowed to be silent about him? And if we were silent, would we then be silent about *God?* Does it not have to be at least a *silence made precise by speech* in order to be truly silence about God?

There are to be sure other situations in our lives where a silence defined by speech is the only possibility. I think of a student in Berlin who was shot to death and of the horrible fact that this incident was only *one* of many such cases. In such situations words fail us. Yet we cannot remain silent, even though silence is the only appropriate response. Grief over the slaying of an innocent person—can it be anything but *a silence defined by speech* if it is not to degenerate into a farce?

Should we not in this sense at least *speak* of God in order that by speaking we would be *more precisely silent* about him? Some Anglo-Saxon scholars (like R. Miles and Th. McPherson), in opposition to the language of "literal theism," have recommended as appropriate for religious expression the language of a "theistic parable." This is the language of a silence brought to expression through similes; i.e. to say, a silence more sharply defined through similes.[18] And there is in the Christian church an ancient and considerable theological tradition that believes it similarly necessary to speak about God as the truly unspeakable—*non ut illud disceretur, sed ne taceretur omnino.*

Nevertheless, Reformation theology, not without reason, rejected this influential theological tradition. The reason was that, were a silence honed by speech the only human stance appropriate to God, then, regardless of however inappropriate, it would be *man* who brings *God* to speech. God

[18] R. Miles, *Religion and the Scientific Outlook* (London, 1959); Thomas McPherson, "Religion and the Inexpressible," *New Essays in Philosophical Theology* (London, 1955). Cf. van Buren, *The Secular Meaning of the Gospel*, p. 91, and Van Austin Harvey, "Die Gottesfrage in der amerikanischen Theologie," *Zeitschrift für Theologie und Kirche*, LXIV (1967), 331.

would be, as it were, an object of man's linguistic capacity, albeit an object against which man's language is again and again condemned to be shattered. Reformation theology responds, to the contrary, that God is not *brought* to speech, but rather *comes* to speech. God is not simply added to man's speech by man himself. But he is also not created by man out of human language. God himself comes to speech. To talk about God in ignorance of his coming to speech is to make an idol of God. In particular, Reformed theology sought to guard itself radically against this attitude: you shall not make yourself a graven image (=you shall let God come to speech). In perfect agreement with this, Lutheran theology emphasized that the assertion "God comes to word" can only be stated because God *has come* to word. The concept of the Word of God, and with it, that of the *deus predicatus*, determine therefore what one could designate as Luther's theological axiom or his fundamental theology. The attempt to engage critically the thesis of the "non-verifiability" of the word "God" shall now be undertaken from within the responsibility demanded of us by Reformation theology.

The verification principle, whose application is supposed to represent the "core of the method of language analysis" is defined more precisely by van Buren in the sense that "the meaning of a word is its use in its context." That is, "the meaning of a statement is to be found in, and is identical with, the function of that statement." With this understanding of verification van Buren refers to the semantic theory of functionalism that represents "a relativizing of logical positivism" and its "intolerant verification principle" that "permits only empirical statements of fact as meaningful linguistic expressions." [19] Van Buren expressly appeals to Ludwig Wittgenstein for his understanding of the semantic theory of functionalism—the meaning of a word is its use in the language. "This thesis and its supporting argument . . . is fundamental to our whole study," maintains van Buren.[20] To what extent this claim is justified, does not interest us here (cf. in this regard Antonin Wagner, O.P., "Ist das Wort 'Gott' tot?"). The results interest us. They run in the direction of maintaining that the empirical element in the language of faith is determined by the relationship of that which is expressed in this language to the *person* of the believer, and not by the connection of that which is expressed to the realm of *facts*. "To introduce the word 'facts' at this point (relative to the language of faith) is to beg for logical confusion and linguistic chaos." The empirical dimension in the language of faith consists of its similarity to the linguistic accessory of human experience, such as the language of love, whose empirical aspect is not to be denied, even though it conveys something other than "facts." "If no family resemblances

[19] Antonin Wagner, O.P., "Ist das Wort 'Gott' tot?" *Freiburger Zeitschrift für Philosophie und Theologie*, 13/14 (1966/67), 94. Cf. van Buren, p. 104.
[20] Van Buren, *The Secular Meaning of the Gospel*, p. 16, n. 23; cf. Wittgenstein, *Philosophical Investigations* (Oxford, 1958), §§ 1-43.

were allowed between the language of the Gospel and the way in which we speak of being loved by another human being, we should have to abandon all hope of understanding what the Gospel means." Accordingly, theological statements are not to be understood as direct empirical affirmations about the world. To the contrary, the verification principle employed by van Buren should show "that theological statements which are meaningless in a secular age when they are taken as straightforward empirical assertions about the world, nevertheless prove to have a use and a meaning [namely] as the expressions of a historical perspective with far-reaching empirical consequences in a man's life." [21] Theological statements prove verifiable in an empirical world by bringing to expression "attitudes" of man that arise from a definite relationship (namely, to Jesus of Nazareth). The human attitudes (or modes of behavior) brought to expression in theological assertions are the empirical proof of a fundamental, basic attitude or perspective that, for its part, arises from a concrete (existential) relationship to Jesus of Nazareth. Van Buren, following R. M. Hare, calls the basic attitude that expresses itself in empirical human attitudes or modes of behavior, a "blik." This is a Dutch word that the English philosopher uses, "strangely enough" [22] in order to express the fact that everyman, in his normal intercourse with the world, is directed by a basic orientation that is not to be explained by external observation (with appeal to David Hume). Everyman has some kind of "blik" that primarily directs his behavior. One does not argue about such bliks;[23] one executes them. According to van Buren, the language of Christian faith is determined by such a "blik," as of course also the activity of those who speak this language. The particular "blik" of the language of Christian faith, and of those who speak it, has its origin in the relationship to Jesus of Nazareth. Precisely, however, in relationship to this Jesus the question of God arises anew. If Jesus was the absolutely "free man," then we must inquire about the origin of his freedom. Who or what makes Jesus to be the one he is—the free man who in his freedom mediates freedom? One can altogether reduce the question about the being of Jesus to this question. That Jesus is the Christ, the Lord, the Word, etc. should in any case also express the fact that true freedom is to be found in him. Nevertheless, who or what makes Jesus the personification of freedom? Who or what makes of Jesus the one whom faith confesses?

The New Testament texts authorize the answering of these questions. They do this, however, not without placing the situation of the questioners in a very particular light. Whoever asks about the being of Jesus receives no answer from the New Testament texts without being himself placed

[21] Van Buren, pp. 105, 199.
[22] As Van Austin Harvey remarked, representing many who, too, are puzzled, *Zeitschrift für Theologie und Kirche*, LXIV (1967), 333.
[23] Cf. van Buren, p. 155.

in a very particular relationship to Jesus. This situation, i.e., its realization in faith, van Buren sought to make relevant by means of his demand to interpret the New Testament assertions as expressions of "a historical perspective with far-reaching empirical consequences in a man's life." And this demand is irrefutable, for one can discern *who* Jesus Christ is only if one senses *how* one relates to Jesus Christ.

Regardless, even this experience, according to the witness of the New Testament, is certainly not to be had without God. One cannot experience how one relates to Jesus Christ without experiencing how one relates to God. For God alone made Jesus to be the one he is; Jesus did not cause himself to be who he is:

> God has made him
> both Lord and Christ,
> this Jesus whom you crucified (Acts 2:36).
> Therefore God has highly exalted him
> and bestowed on him the name
> which is above every name (Phil. 2:9).

An answer authorized by the New Testament to the question of who Jesus is—i.e., what it is that makes him the one whom faith confesses—cannot be ascertained with the contexts of an empirical world; no more than it could be ascertained from within the context of an idealistically conceived world. An answer authorized by the New Testament to the question of who Jesus is continues (precisely because this answer implies the experience of our relationship to Jesus Christ) to rely on the use of the word "God." Whoever understands Jesus Christ experiences the one described by the word "God" as the one of whom one is compelled to speak. But that is exactly what van Buren had contested. For him the word "God" is no longer a word in our language because it will not submit to empirical verification.

Behind this view probably stands, as a premise, the statement of the early Wittgenstein: "The limits of my speech mean the limits of my world." [24] In the context of the *Tractatus*, this sentence becomes theologically relevant by the contention that "God does not reveal himself *in* the world." Although the "limits of the world" are thought by the Wittgenstein of the *Tractatus* to be alterable, so that "the world as a whole can, so to say, decrease or increase," [25] God remains nevertheless *fundamentally outside* the limits of my world which are discernible in the limits of my language. Accordingly, God belongs to that type of phenomenon about which one

---

[24] *Tractatus logico-philosophicus* 5.6. Van Buren does not draw upon the *Tractatus* for his language analysis, but rather on the *Philosophical Investigations* which revoke various theses of the *Tractatus*. Even so, the contention that the limits of my language designate the limits of my world, seems to me, if by "language" one understands the manifold of possible functioning "language games," to be the factual premise of the statements.

[25] *Ibid.*, 6.43.

cannot speak. And "concerning that about which man cannot speak, man must be silent." [26]

These propositions, consciously or unconsciously presupposed in the appearance of the modern death-of-God-theology, are a challenge to a confrontation in which the dialogue of the Christian faith with the language of the world must today prove itself. The confrontation is not so much with the "philosophy" of the early Wittgenstein as it is with the world view that manifests itself in its use. All the while we concur with the premise that the limits of our speech signify the limits of our world.

V

Within the limits of our language the word "God" belongs to our language only when it functions to signify an operation within the limits of our world. On the other hand, to talk of God makes sense only when the function of the word "God" within our language is clear and irreplaceable, so that it cannot be replaced by the function of another word, so that no other function within the limits of our world can take over the function indicated by the word "God." Yet, where can it be proved that the word "God" so works in our language that it indicates such an irreplaceable function within the limits of our world? Whom should we question concerning this matter?

Is the answer to be found within our language as such and its limits which indicate the limits of the world? That would mean that the word "God" functions in our language, as it were, in a natural way. When man understands himself as ζῷον λόγον ἔχον, when he understands himself as the linguistic being, he could also understand that the word "God" says something or that it says nothing. Nevertheless, in contradistinction to this there is the fact that the word "God" becomes clear to Christian faith only in the context of a word event that, while of course occurring only within the limits of our language, yet is as such not a word event which is part of our language, but rather is the event of the Word of God. Christian faith understands the God designated by the word "God" as the one who speaks, as the one who speaks from and out of himself. As such God himself gives the word "God" its function within the limits of our speech, namely, to let the God who speaks of his own accord come to speech.

Thus it would not be for our language, and the world with its limits as designated by the limits of our language, to decide if the word "God" were still a word in our language. Rather, the word "God" becomes a word of our language when and only when the Word of God is already functioning within the limits of our language and that is when God has spoken of his own accord. It is the Word of God already functioning within the limits of our language that is not only *sui ipsius interpres,* but also interpreter of

[26] *Ibid.,* p. 7.

the function of the word "God" in our language. Only the Word of God functioning within the limits of our language gives answer to the question: Who is God that we *must* speak of him? [27] The use of the word "God" depends on a prior hearing in order to let God come to speech as the one who speaks of his own accord.

Consequently, the question of whether "God" is still a word in our language leads back to the question of the function of the *Word of God* in our language. The failure to return to this question leads either to unjustifiably continued talk about God or to unjustifiably continued silence about God. Whoever, without justification, continues to talk about God in avoidance of the Word of God, talks God to death. And whoever, avoiding the Word of God, forgoes talk about God, silences God to death. In order that God be neither talked to death nor silenced to death, the Word of God demands undivided linguistic attention.

VI

The formulation "Word of God" claims to do something within the limits of our language that this language of ours cannot do of itself. Word of God is thus not simply information about something, since our language is able, by its own power, to give information about that which is and occurs within the limits of our world. And it cannot be the task of a word that functions within the limits of our language (limits that also designate the limits of our world) to provide information about something beyond our world; this is true also for the Word of God. Therefore an informing function alone cannot exhaust the function of the Word of God in our language. Rather, the Word of God claims, as it informs, to do something additional. It *judges*. Just as a legal judgment does not only give information about the handing down of a legal decision, but also publicly enforces this information (guilty, or innocent, as the case may be), so the Word of God functions in our language "living and active, sharper than any two-edged sword, piercing to the division of soul and spirit, of joints and marrow, and discerning the thoughts and intentions of the heart" (Heb. 4:12). When God's Word about Jesus Christ reports who he is and how we are related to him, it not only informs us, but also empowers within the limits of our language and our world this narrative as history.

As a report about Jesus Christ the Word of God does not lead us beyond the boundaries of our language and our world; rather it directs us exclusively to the world indicated by the limits of our language judging it at the same time. Whoever judges, makes distinctions. As the report about

[27] "God" as a word of our language is certainly always the word of a text. Whoever would understand God can therefore not follow the spirit without giving praise to the letter, the letter that indeed kills without the spirit, but without which, nevertheless, the spirit does not make alive.

Jesus Christ the Word of God is that judgment which functions within the limits of our language and thus of our world as the *absolutely decisive court*. What is decided? In his letter to the Romans, Paul writes concerning God's promise to the Jews: "What if some were unfaithful? Does their faithlessness nullify the faithfulness of God? By no means! Let God be true though every man be false, as it is written" (Rom. 3:3-4).

God's Word is regarded here as the word that decides not only between truth and falsehood, but also at the same time between God and man. In this way the Word of God understands its own special function in our language and in our world. It functions within the limits of our language and within the limits of the world designated by that language by establishing its limit *within the limits* of our language. What kind of a limit? It is not a limit that sets boundaries or confines the language (as for example countries or states are bounded) or divides it (as a boundary can divide a country). Rather, it is a limit that in the use of language drives toward linguistic differentiation. The limit defined in our language by the Word of God compels a differentiation that determines our use of language, totally and at all times, namely, the differentiation between the only true God and all mankind who cannot be made true except by this only true God. Insofar as the Word of God thus describes its wholly distinctive limit within the limits of our language, it makes the word "God," in its differentiation from all other words of our language, function meaningfully within our language.

This settles it that the suspicion as to the meaninglessness of the word "God" can indeed be rejected only within the limits of our language, but always and only by the Word of God itself. The Word of God operating within the limits of our language rejects this suspicion, but only indirectly, namely insofar as it makes positive use of the word "God." The Word of God makes positive use of the word "God" in speaking of God and in claiming truth for its speech. The problem of the meaninglessness, namely, the unimportance of the word "God," becomes thereby the question of the truth of our talk about God. It raises the basic problem of verification. If one wishes to take it seriously, then it is indispensible to distinguish between the truth of a sentence (subject—predicate) and the truth as event (the truth will make you free; I am the way, and the truth, and the life; John 8:32; 14:6), in order then to ask about the connection between the truth of a statement and the truth of an event.

In agreement with logical positivism one must proceed from the premise that there are no true or false words. Thus also the word "God," as a separate word of our language, can be neither true nor false. Certainly the word "God" also does not simply enter into the realm of truth by being employed in sentences (logical judgments) which then permit of verification. There are in this sense no true theological sentences at all, because truth understood theologically does not permit of measurement by a positivistically understood criterion of truth. Nevertheless, there is a certain formal analogy to logical positivism in that only in very distinct *linguistic contexts* does the word "God" enter that realm where, although the mere word "God" can certainly never be true therein, nevertheless the naming, the saying, the invocation of this word can indeed become true. "God" is a word of invocation ("My God, my God, why hast thou forsaken me"). Therefore truth from a theological perspective first of all has to be viewed as an event. In this sense it is true that certain linguistic contexts under certain conditions are so related to the event of truth that they themselves become true and may claim to be true.

Insofar as this claim to truth formulates itself, it results in apophantic subject-predicate sentences that participate in the claimed "truth as event" in the form of a propositional truth. The problem of such propositional truths resides in the fact that they represent only a *being* true, and thereby fail to point out that this being true really involves the absolutizing of a *becoming* true. The problem here is that of the formation of dogma. The true theological proposition threatens always to outflank the truth as event, and to this extent it is inevitably and always at the point of becoming untrue. But what is that—truth as event? Where is truth event?

VII

Truth as event is accessible only in the context of language, or more precisely, only in particular linguistic relationships. We cannot determine from the context of language as such which linguistic relationships would be appropriate in this instance. The language we speak gives us no concrete indications as to how truth as event is to be encountered. Truth as event encounters us of its own accord. Its conditions can be known only from encounters which have already occurred.

When truth is encountered as event what is at stake is *time*. When truth is encountered as event, time can be taken, but can also be given. For truth occurs, and thus *uses* time—time, for example, that could have been used for lying. Truth occurs, of course, in such a way that it reaches out beyond the time of its own occurrence, since it is *truth* that is occurring and as such raises a claim beyond its own moment. Truth as encounter accuses and acquits; it pertains to the past and the future.

Inasmuch as it accuses it takes away time that belonged to me. Before a court, for example, the criminal's time (during and beyond the time of the crime) becomes public time, time that no longer belongs to him in any respect, and in consequence of which a decision now denies him future time as his time. The same sort of thing occurs not only before the court, but whenever truth encounters us as event in an accusing way.

Correspondingly and conversely, it is also true that truth as event can encounter us as acquittal, thereby granting me time that does not belong to me as yet. Insofar as truth as event denies and grants time it is a language event. Language events are not simply events *in* time, but rather events *determining* (granting or consuming) *time.*

Truth as event is not a specific theological category nor a specific theological phenomenon. Wherever there is life it appears, and wherever there is thought, it can be comprehended. Understood theologically, truth as event is the predicate of another event that we called the event of the Word of God.

VIII

The event of the Word of God is characterized by the fact that it is not a priori identical with any human linguistic context, least of all with the context of human language (or languages) in general, and that nevertheless it is encountered only in human linguistic relationships and thus within the context of human language as such. When it so occurs, then truth as event encounters us in it. The event of the Word of God within the limits of our language brings with it its own truth. And our talk about God, our linguistic use of the word "God," becomes true insofar as it reaches into the realm of this truth and consequently into the context of the Word of God. To reach the realm of this truth means nothing other than to expose oneself to the limit that God's Word establishes within the limits of our language.

The truth claim of such talk about God—talk that is always merely *becoming* true—subsequently finds formulation in theological assertions (as, e.g., the dogmas). Their sole danger is that they are only too true and that they can thus easily be misunderstood to the point of not permitting of being proved false under any circumstances.

In reply to such misunderstanding it should be stated that only such theological sentences can reasonably claim to be true as really expose themselves to the conflict between true and false and therefore do not in principle exclude the possibility of being falsified. An assertion that can under no circumstances be proved false can also not be true, since it does not even make sense. Every positive judgment must be able to exclude certain facts as not being compatible with it; that is, it must be able to name conditions under which it would be possible to prove it false. Are theological propositions in this sense not falsifiable and therefore also simply not true? [28]

The opposite is the case, since theological assertions include faithlessness as the fact that contradicts their truth any time. Every theological judgment

[28] It is certainly useful to point out that these propositions, formulated in clear analogy to Popper's postulate of falsifiability, neither raise the claim to satisfy this postulate of empirical falsifiability, nor make the attempt to compete with this postulate on the same level.

designates (*de facto*) unbelief as the condition under which it could be proved false. If nevertheless a theological assertion should wish to maintain that its truth is compatible with the contradicting fact of unbelief, then this contention may be regarded as meaningless. Thereby the problem of falsification is certainly radicalized, insofar as unbelief contradicts *in every respect* the truth represented in theological assertions. That in turn is based on the fact that the truth represented in theological assertions implies a totality, that it *speaks* in every respect. Every theological statement is not only falsifiable, but is continuously exposed to the struggle of being true or false. For the *being* true that these statements represent always refers back to a *becoming* true that has its own time. We call this time the time of faith. Its peculiarity consists in the fact that it alone helps the Word of God establish its limits within the limits of our speech and thus lets our use of the word "God" become authentic. Since our use of the word "God" becomes authentic only in faith, true talk about God always provokes a conflict about its own truth. Luther expressed this when he understood God's revelation in our world as a being revealed *sub contrario*. Only faith understands that which conceals itself under the contradiction as a contradiction of the contradiction, that which offers itself under the foolishness of the word of Jesus' death on the cross as the wisdom of God that leads to life.

This means, however, that the Word of God verifies the use of the word "God" within the limits of our language *secundum hominem* only in such a way that it verifies the verification *secundum deum*. God's Word makes our talk about God so true among us that it proves us to be liars who, as men, can be made true only by God. Where the verification of the Word of God is at stake and, related to it, the verification of our talk about God, the conflict about the *verum facere* is bound to develop.[29] The point of contact between the opponents is constituted by the fact that this conflict is carried on within the limits of our language. Theology has to verify its truth at this point of contact by justifying the function of the Word of God within the limits of our language *secundum dicentem deum*. It must do this in such a way that it equally resists a positivistic verification principle on the one hand, and a verificationless revelation positivism on the other. It does this in giving its undivided attention to the limit that God's Word establishes within the limits of our language, and thereby grants that time which alone aids in the establishment of this limit: the time of faith. For the Word of God does not set its limit within the limits of our language without thereby helping faith come to speech. Faith owes itself to the establishment of the boundary that distinguishes within the limits of our language between the authentic God and man, who is to be made authentic by God alone. For the believer, and only he, is the man who, although a liar, has

[29] Gerhard Ebeling has worked through the facts of this situation beautifully.

been made true by the only true God. Only in faith and its speech does God verify himself. The only true God makes himself true in our midst in making us, liars that we are, true; and God makes us true by bringing us to faith and so causing us to speak of God.

IX

A verification of God outside of faith is out of the question—because of who we are. It would make God untrue and leave us untrue. God and faith belong together—as Luther not only inculcated in his catechism, but also elaborated in his exegesis. A case in point is his exegetical paraphrase of Romans 3:4: *"Est enim Deus verax; ergo ei credendum. Omnis autem homo mendax; ergo ei non credendum nec sequendum."* [30]

The meaning of the truth that God and faith belong together cannot be fathomed. Luther went so far as to call *fides* the *creatrix divinitatis non in persona, sed in nobis.* That is an exalted conception, but not *too* exalted. It is in any case correct that faith makes man, who is not to be trusted, trustworthy, since faith not only distinguishes God from man, but also makes God, who is forever different from man, appear in our manhood. Faith proves God right among us and in us. And thereby it gives God room among us and in us. Yet, how should God find room in us?

Faith gives God room among and in us by letting man be distinguished not only from God, but also from himself. It is not true that faith makes man identical with himself. The sinner wants to become identical with himself. The believer does not distinguish himself from the sinner by having finally achieved identity with himself; rather he distinguishes himself by no longer being in need of becoming identical with himself. As a believer I bear the distinction of man from himself by letting God dwell between me and myself. The believer lives by the distinction that the Word of God has made, not only in our language, but in man as a linguistic being. The power of this distinction is the *plus* of faith. A man who distinguishes gets more out of life.

X

In conclusion we want to clarify the foregoing by paying attention to the information which the Word of God enforces when it reports who Jesus Christ is and how we are related to him. To this end we appeal once more to the apostle Paul. In II Cor. 4 he speaks of himself with a strange differentiation. For reasons we will presently indicate, he says: "So we do not lose heart. Though our outer nature is wasting away, our inner nature is being renewed every day. For this slight momentary affliction is preparing for us an eternal weight of glory beyond all comparison, because we

---

[30] Weimar Edition LVI, 225, 2-3.

look not to the things that are seen but to the things that are unseen; for the things that are seen are transient, but the things that are unseen are eternal" (II Cor. 4:16-18). All this sounds slightly platonic, is in fact permeated with Hellenistic concepts, and yet forecloses the possibility of being understood if one seeks to understand it on these grounds. Paul rather speaks by virtue of that distinction that is the *plus* of faith. For this reason he does not lose heart. For the apostle carries with him and in himself, wherever he goes, the power of the differentiation that the Word of God effects as a boundary within the limits of our language and our world. And that gives him ever new strength in his weakness, so that he can continue to carry this power with him further, and bring it, as God's power, among the people. "We have this treasure in earthen vessels, to show that the transcendent power belongs to God and not to us. We are afflicted in every way, but not crushed; perplexed, but not driven to despair; persecuted, but not forsaken; struck down, but not destroyed" (II Cor. 4:7-9).

In this strange differentiation of the apostolic existence there appears bodily what the apostle has to say about his Lord Jesus Christ. Just as the apostle has to proclaim the Word of the cross, so he had to carry in his own body the dying and the death of the crucified Jesus, so that also the life of Jesus might be revealed bodily. What the apostle has to say becomes powerfully visible in his own body. The information the apostle has to communicate shapes his own existence. "The dead Jesus—he is the living Lord," is what the apostle has to say. And because the living Lord is forever identical with this dead Jesus, the existence of the apostle as formed by the Lord must forever be distinct. For we are "always carrying in the body the death of Jesus, so that the life of Jesus may also be manifested in our bodies" (II Cor. 4:10). Through the distinction between death and life the existence of the apostle makes manifest that only God can so overcome the difference between life and death that men must say of one who is dead: he lives. Therefore we have the treasure of the gospel, the treasure of the report of what can be said about Jesus Christ, in earthen vessels, so that the transcendent powers should betray its origins as God's and not ours.

Thus, whoever thinks he can speak of Jesus Christ without having to speak of God, ignores the fact that the Jesus who affects us is a dead person. Whoever thinks he can speak about how we are related to Jesus without thereby having to talk about God, ignores the fact that the life of Jesus seeks to be revealed in our sufferings. That which occurs in the physical sufferings of the apostle is an event of proclamation that maintains the unity of Jesus' cross and God's glory,[31] so that the *existence* of the apostle makes the word "God" indispensable and necessary. Referring to a psalm,

[31] Concerning this point in its entirety, cf. E. Güttgemanns, *Der leidende Apostel und sein Herr. Studien zur paulinischen Christologie:* FRLANT 90 (Göttingen, 1966), 94-124.

"I believed, and so I spoke" (Ps. 116:10), the apostle continues the interpretation of his apostolic existence:

> we too believe,
> and so we speak,
> knowing that
> he who raised the Lord Jesus
> will raise us also with Jesus
> and bring us with you into his presence.
> For it is all for your sake,
> so that as grace extends to more and more people
> [i.e., the believing, who must speak]
> it may increase thanksgiving,
> to the glory of God. (II Cor. 4:13-15)

Apostolic existence causes, as it were, the word "God" to burst out, but the necessity to speak of God is not at all limited to the apostle. Just as it is *God* who made Jesus who he is, so it is God again who makes us what we will be and now already are, namely, those who *live* in the face of death with Jesus Christ. In view of the passing of his life's time the believer experiences an eternal time gain. This news must be spread among the people, so that more and more might come to faith.

Where this message finds faith, every mouth opens up in thanksgiving to God. Through giving thanks the differentiation realized by the Word of God becomes concrete in human words. For one who gives thanks differentiates—or else he prattles. And it is the ultimate goal of all apostolic activity to further God's glory through thanksgiving. All depends on *God's* coming to word whenever we, through God's Word, receive the power of faith and thus of speech. When faith happens, there is an eternal time gain that articulates itself in a temporal speech gain: increasing grace lets thanksgiving abound to the glory of God. In thanksgiving, the word "God" finds expression in speech when the Word of God defines its limit within the limits of our language.

Thus we have found an answer to our question: Who is God that we *must* speak about him? God is he whom man must give thanks. More exactly, God is he whom we cannot thank enough. The fact that we cannot thank him *enough* defines him as the one whom we must fear above all else. The fact that we cannot *thank* him enough defines him as the one one whom we may love above all things. Thus we are told how we stand with God when we experience how we stand with Jesus Christ. At the same time we are told how we stand with ourselves. If *God is* the one whom *we* cannot thank enough, everything is also said about us that needs to be said.

Once again: Is the word "God" still a word of our language? Answer: "God" can always only *become* a word that speaks of God.

II

FROM THE WORD TO THE WORDS*

Karl Barth and the Tasks of Practical Theology

HANS-DIETER BASTIAN

When Karl Barth unleashed his dialectic of the Word of God and the words of man, he undoubtedly made what for the church and for theology was to become the most momentous decision of the twentieth century. Here lies the basis for the present discussions of the hermeneutic problem, and here terminate the polemics about a new homiletics, a new system of catechetical instruction and so forth. Just as the English physicist Eddington once asked Lord Rutherford, whether he had discovered or made his model of the atom, it seems appropriate to inquire theologically: Did Karl Barth find and discover his dialectic between the Word of God and human words, or did he invent and make it? The answer is closely related to the history and origin of the problem itself. For this problem does not acutely arise in the guild of professional theologians or in an academic tradition but in the vocational experience of the pastor in the territorial state church. Hans Joachim Iwand sees the situation quite similarly: "He [Barth] hit upon this problem not because he was doing research, but because he had to preach! Here in the realm of practical theology a question arose, a kind of being-at-a-loss, for which professional theology simply had no answer." [1] The expression "in the realm of practical theology" in Iwand's statement

* Translated by Reinhard Ulrich, Lakeland College, Sheboygan, Wisconsin, from *Evangelische Theologie,* 28:1 (January, 1968), pp. 25-55.

[1] H. Gollwitzer, W. Kreck, K-G. Steck, E. Wolf, eds. H. J. Iwand, *Nachgelassene Werke* I, (Munich, 1962), p. 185.

needs clarification. We certainly may not take this to mean the youngest of the classical theological university disciplines. As shall be shown later, an erosion of the borderline between practical theology (understood as theological-ecclesiastical practice) and Practical Theology (understood as an academic discipline) can only lead to devastating results, which cannot be prevented, even if an attempt is made to mark the borderline by way of orthography. At any rate, Barth's Word-words dialectic has come to light as a specifically pastoral problem of preaching and not as a contribution of practical theology. "The well-known problem of the pastor at his desk on Saturday and in the pulpit on Sunday coalesced for me into that marginal note to all of theology." [2] From his vantage point of practical proclamation Karl Barth spells out the question: What does it mean to preach?—not pragmatically: How is it done? but dogmatically: How can it be done? [3] Since the pastoral act of preaching lacked an assertory foundation, the preacher Barth became the dogmatic theologian, who with his formula of the Word of God delineated for academic theology its task and for the church's proclamation its criterion. Barth boldly generalized his own problem as a pastor into the fundamental question of the church's teaching as such, drew a line from his own pulpit to all pulpits and from there to the professorship of dogmatics, made this direction the direction of his entire life work, and methodologically restated his pastoral scruples as the basic program of *Church Dogmatics*: "The task of dogmatics then is an inquiry into the church's proclamation with regard to its agreement with the Word of God, with regard to its appropriateness to that which it wants to proclaim. . . . In dogmatics the church makes itself liable to that which in its proclamation it has undertaken. It puts this undertaking to the test by facing it critically, suspending for a moment that claim and expectation insofar as in reflection it separates its proclamation from the Word of God, so that it can measure, not the Word of God by its proclamation, but its proclamation by the Word of God." [4] Barth's doctrine of the threefold form of the Word of God, extensively developed in *Church Dogmatics* I/1, is designed to fulfill the intent of dogmatics to render problematic a naïve identification of the church's proclamation with the Word of God in a sincere attempt to verify the relationship given here. "Dogmatics examines the church's language about God with regard to the question whether as word of man it is fit for service of the Word of God." [5] This examination takes place as a "passage from the Bible to the sermon";[6] it informs the preacher of what he must say

[2] Karl Barth, "Not und Verheissung der christlichen Verkündigung" (1922), *Das Wort Gottes und die Theologie* (Munich, 1924), p. 101.

[3] *Ibid.*, p. 103.

[4] Karl Barth, *Kirchliche Dogmatik*, I/1, 263-64. [Translator's note: trans. of this and all following passages of KD mine.]

[5] *Ibid.*, I/2, 874.

[6] *Ibid.*, I/2, 865.

and assures him that the cause he represents is not his own but God's. The Word-words dialectic is primarily a problem of the theological reassurance of the pastoral function. It is tied up with the obedience by which the preacher knows himself in duty bound and constitutes an expression of the reflection with which he actively practices that obedience. The question of the relationship between the Word and the words does not arise in a neutral research situation, but for Barth it is tied to the kerygma: "[It is] not primarily the question of a student, who is concerned about an agreement of his ideas with the superior ideas of his teacher, but it is primarily the question of a servant, who is obliged to ask whether his actions agree with the intentions of his Lord, who may then and on that occasion certainly find something to learn which he did not know before." [7] Nevertheless, the doctrine of the Word of God does not belong in the pulpit but in the academic classroom. It is a task of theological reflection and, like all academic productions, in need of critical examination.

Here it is disturbing to note the universal claim made by the Word-words doctrine. Since the reality of the Word of God sovereignly determines the reality of the church's words, Barth demands that dogmatics be given the central position in theology. He equates good or bad dogmatics with good or bad theology and with good or bad preaching.[8] Dogmatics, thus founded apodictically upon the Word, develops a kind of pull which absorbs all other theological disciplines. Consequently, Barth finds it difficult to sort these out again theoretically. He reserves the problem of the form of the church's proclamation for practical theology,[9] but he also leaves no doubt that the real decisions in the matter have already been made by dogmatics in terms of questions of content. Dogmatics alone brings about the previously mentioned passage from the Bible to the sermon. Dogmatics encourages proclamation, and it does this in such impressive fashion that many a preacher hit upon the quite plausible idea of exploiting the *Church Dogmatics* for everyday use. The perceptive among them however soon realized that they had fallen victim to a hearing error.[10] The real intent and the substantive accomplishment of Barth's doctrine of the Word lies in the fact that it deals seriously with the problem of certainty for the preacher. It is therefore not surprising that this doctrine became irreplaceably significant and effective wherever that certainty was threatened and endangered. As is well known, the past reveals many instances of this in the history of the church. But we are not considering here the difficulties Barth has solved, but those which he has not solved or those which he has in fact created.

[7] *Ibid.,* I/1, 289-90.
[8] *Ibid.,* I/2, 858.
[9] *Ibid.,* I/2, 857.
[10] M. Storch, *Exegesen und Meditationen zu K. Barths Kirchl. Dogmatik* (Munich, 1964), pp. 195-96.

The universal claim of the dogmatic doctrine of the Word tolerated practical theology only as a matter of paraphrase. The homiletical and catechetical projects, which have been developed in the context of the *Church Dogmatics*, may easily serve to show how difficult it was for their authors to preserve the methodological autonomy of their questions and answers. The universal key of the Word of God simply fits every theological lock—or so it seems, and opens every church door—or so it seems. It does so however only as long as one accepts the Word-words dialectic as the model key. Contemporary practical theology could cite some weighty reasons why we should refrain from doing so, foremost among them the following: The doctrine of the Word of God permits the chasm between the dogmatic claims of proclamation and its painful reality context to grow ever deeper. It one-sidedly reassures him who speaks in the church, but widely ignores him who hears in the church, particularly if the latter is no longer able or willing to hear and to be "churchly," or if he has ultimately decided to emigrate from the sermon-preaching church. The dogmatic passage, which begins with the Bible text and terminates in the sermon, consistently overlooks that spoken communication moves beyond the preacher to the hearer and that it may be examined in terms of its effects or non-effects. The claim of the sermon would necessarily have to be relegated to its real situation. But this is accomplished neither by dogmatics nor by the Word-words dialectic.

The doctrine of the Word could not prevent and may even have encouraged, in the judgment of quite diverse theologians, that the concept of the sermon was enthusiastically exaggerated,[11] that the talk about proclamation has almost been emptied of content, and that the traditional equation of the sermon and the Word of God is in danger of a fundamental breakup. The essay by Wolfgang Trillhaas, "Die wirkliche Predigt," [12] describes nothing less than a state of emergency.[13] It tells of a real situation in view of which the doctrine of the sovereign Word could only constitute a deceptive calm, when in fact no one who is concerned with the issue has a right to be tranquil. "It is an illusion that every ordained man in the present Protestant Church should *eo ipso* also be a preacher and that every so-called sermon delivered somewhere today should *eo ipso facto* be the 'Word of God.' " [14] Similar to Trillhaas in its disillusioning effect is Helmut Thielicke's understanding of the crisis in preaching: "Our word in the sermon merely shares the fateful impotency of all other words." [15]

[11] D. Rössler, "Das Problem der Homiletik," ThPr I:1 (1966), 21.
[12] Wolfgang Trillhaas, "Die wirkliche Predigt," in H. Gerdes, ed., *Wahrheit und Glaube. Festschrift für E. Hirsch* (Itzehoe, 1963), pp. 193 ff.
[13] *Ibid.*, p. 195: "The majority of the public sermons in Protestant churches are homiletical trivialities."
[14] *Ibid.*, p. 197.
[15] H. Thielicke, "Leiden an der Kirche," *Stundenbuch* 52 (Hamburg, 1965/66). Cf. the following chapters: "The Mess of Preaching," "The Preacher as Helpless Soloist," "The Decay of the Language of Preaching."

Here practical theology clearly reaches a fork in the road. *Either* it follows Karl Barth and subordinates the wretchedness of the church's acting and speaking to the one and only proper criterion, the Word of God. In that case it will be unable to do anything but invoke the evidence of the Word-words dialectic homiletically, catechetically, or in whatever other fashion.[16] Faced with desparate experiences of proclamation, which in fact exist, it will even more desparately conjure up the reality of the Word of God, which in the area of secular language does not exist, at least not in the same manner as human words exist. Recently Barth's student and interpreter Walter Kreck emphasized once again the axiomatic character of the Word of God and pointed out that its unique modus of reality can never be judged by our way of looking at reality, but that it can be grasped only in a christological-trinitarian context. "The reality of the Word of God cannot be predicated in the same way as the reality of what exists [das Seiende]." [17] In such a dialectic of heterogenous realities—a divine and a human one, a powerful and a powerless one—practical theology would be driven back and forth helplessly: It would be paralyzed on both sides, unable to determine the Word of God, that obstinately triumphant "thing-in-itself," [18] and unqualified to liberate the human word from its impotency.

As we have said, *either* practical theology follows the doctrine of the Word and gains certainty dogmatically, but loses reality practically, *or* it turns away from the axiomatic Word to human words, accepts the responsibility for their power and powerlessness and subjects the church's speaking and acting to radical empirical analysis. This second way, which we would like to commend, has a number of consequences at least two of which must be discussed right at the outset. First, by abstaining from an axiomatic understanding of the Word of God practical theology loses ultimate theological certainty. It forgoes the possibility of formulating assertory sentences and becomes hypothetical.[19] For heuristic reasons it will have to treat all theological disciplines, including dogmatics, as auxiliary disciplines. Practical theology then is not the marketplace where the results of exegesis are exchanged; it does not provide the desired opportunity to give an appro-

---

[16] M. Mezger, "Die Amtshandlungen der Kirche als Verkündigung," *Ordnung und Seelsorge* I (Munich, 1963, 2nd ed), 61: "It is a mute question, whether the word has the power to get a hold of men. If the word is about the business of proclamation, then it does get a hold of men. The proper measure of the kerygmatic authority and pneumatic power of proclamation is not worn-out and depraved preaching, but preaching which counts on the promise of *exousia*."

[17] W. Kreck, "Die Wirklichkeit des Wortes Gottes," ThExh NF 134 (Munich, 1966), 7.

[18] Iwand, *Nachgelassene Werke* I, 185.

[19] *Ibid.*, p. 279: "Historical and practical theology can proceed assertorically insofar as they are not ashamed of their connections with dogmatic theology. Taken by themselves they are hypothetical."

priate shape to dogmatic contents. Rather it is the possibility, attested by definite methods, of locating ecclesiastical and theological activities under the horizon of empirical cognition. Second, and this consequence follows immediately: Practical theology cannot avoid moving next door to the emiprical sciences, which presently have at their disposal the methods capable of opening up the horizons of empirical cognition. But this reorientation of practical theology will succeed only, if practical theology agrees to participate in the now widely held discussions about the place of the sciences (*Wissenschaften*). The guiding motifs here are theory and practice. If they are adopted, we cast ourselves off from the wholeness of a dogmatic confessional base and approach "that uncertain, highly abstract system of hypotheses into which in today's scientific research the rationality of the world's objects is compressed." [20] Let no one misunderstand: we are not pleading for a substitution of the Word of God by the modern scientific consciousness. Neither do we intend vicariously to replace the doctrine of the Word with something else in the fashion of "culture-Protestantism." [21] We are not concerned with an abolition of the Word-words dialectic in dogmatics, but with its heuristically necessary suspension in practical theology. The dogmatic question of the power of the Word of God is here methodologically overshadowed by the empirical question of the power of the church's speaking and acting. This is not a mere whim but arises from the insight, which must be respected dogmatically as well, that the church's speaking and acting can theologically be justified only if they are also acceptable as human speaking and acting. The widely lamented inability of the church to speak out, and the disorientation of its actions, are not to be explained merely as contingent problems of the Word of God, but also as a deficit in the ecclesiastical-theological human sphere. This deficit can only be covered if we deliberately turn toward the sciences, which in their theories concern themselves with the various apparent forms of the human sphere. There is some concern that this might lead to an inglorious dissolution of theology into humanism. But one can fear this only, if philosophically one recognizes the traditional dichotomy of the natural sciences and the humanities and anxiously pays attention to the dualism of diverse subject matters, which can *either* be merely described *or* merely understood. The category of *understanding* has haunted the castle of theology from way back, and it fears nothing so much as being caught by a sober explanation. "Here I would like to indicate my suspicion, that the form of contemporary philosophy might be that of the natural sciences after all, and that we delude ourselves, if we still think it possible to maintain the old philosophy of the word in any form whatever. May it not simply be that the approaches to a new

[20] H. Schelsky, *Einsamkeit und Freiheit. Idee und Gestalt der deutschen Universität und ihrer Reformen* (Hamburg, 1963), 286.
[21] Cf. Barth, *Kirchliche Dogmatik*, I/1, 264-65.

philosophy are to be found with Einstein and Heisenberg, and not with Heidegger? We have gotten too much into the habit of considering the results of the natural sciences as peripheral matters, as information about a non-mental or mechanical world." [22] This suspicion of the dramatist Friedrich Dürrenmatt for years has been part of the theory of science and has been dealt with constructively there. Already a generation ago, Max Scheler called modern German philosophy an achievement primarily of the Protestant parsonage, which "serves to explain some of its substantive characteristics, for example, its relatively loose ties to mathematics and the natural sciences, its apolitical, contemplative spirit, its lack of radicalism, . . . its almost complete inner estrangement from the 'spirit' of industry and technology." [23] Practical theology, which is serious about dealing with the guiding motifs of theory and practice, cannot but note that there is no fundamental difference between the logic of empirical research and that of the natural sciences.[24]

This common logic protests against an unfruitful recapitulation of purely speculative principles in places where exact knowledge of the realities is either completely lacking or has been prematurely skipped over. Problems of practical theology therefore cannot be solved by paraphrasing principal dogmatic utterances homiletically or catechetically. To the contrary, here the logic of the empirical with its hostility toward purely speculative principles provides an invaluable service for theology: It renders futile those countless attempts of providing a veneer of reality for completely empty formulations by dogmatically hypostatizing them, a reality which *de facto* they simply do not possess. It is necessary to mediate logically and critically between the pounding postulate of dogmatics: "Thus preaching must be a kind of pentecostal miracle in miniature," [25] and a sober acknowledgment of the real situation: "The misery of preaching—the erosion of the language of preaching." [26] The doctrine of the Word of God does not get us any further here, even if with Jürgen Moltmann we understand this Word not merely incarnationally (Barth) but "first of all eschatologically." The enigmatic sentence: "The disparity of Word and reality . . . is overcome only in the resurrection of the crucified One" [27] clarifies neither language nor method

[22] F. Dürrenmatt, *Theaterschriften und Reden* (Zürich, 1966), p. 58.
[23] M. Scheler, *Die Wissensformen und die Gesellschaft* (Berne-Munich, 1960), p. 90.
[24] Cf. H. Albert, "Probleme der Wissenschaftslehre in der Sozialforschung," in R. König, ed., *Handbuch der empirischen Sozialforschung*, I (Stuttgart, 1962), 38 ff. Also, H. Arendt, "Natur und Geschichte," *Fragwürdige Traditionsbestände im politischen Denken der Gegenwart* (Frankfurt, 1957), pp. 47 ff. H. Arendt interprets the differences in method between the two research areas as "foreground phenomenon." In regard to the basic problem, cf. K. Gründer, "Hermeneutik und Wissenschaftstheorie," *Philosophisches Jahrbuch*, 75:1 (Munich, 1967), 152 ff.
[25] J. Moltmann, "Wort Gottes und Sprache," MPTh 54:10 (1965), 397.
[26] Thielicke, *Stundenbuch* 52, 11 ff., 53 ff.
[27] Moltmann, "Wort Gottes und Sprache," p. 396.

for a man who has to prepare a sermon or plan a lesson. It merely leads the less gifted to trust the jargon of pure speculation, to stage an "ascension of the Word beyond the realm of the factual, conditional and questionable," and to act, "as if blessings from above were automatically built into this approach." [28]

The logic of empirical research is bound to have the same salutory effect in practical theology as the method of historical criticism has had in exegesis. Just as the latter removed the magic from the biblical text and destroyed the dogma of verbal inspiration, so the former removes the magic from the practical actions of the church and destroys the dogma of the sacramental "binding value" ("*Bannwert*") [29] of the sermon. The research principle and the effect of eleminating magic in the world generally move hand in hand. Protestant theology, which in the last decades has said many kind things about the process of secularization, is hardly in a position to oppose the use of secular methods when it comes to practical theology. If and only if this is done, practical theology will become what theologically it must become: "A court of appeals against self-satisfied speculation." [30]

An exodus from the realm of the traditional humanities and a fruitful contact with the problems of the empirical sciences will induce practical theology to ask questions, which are less interested in the *What* and *Why* and more in the *How* of things. Hannah Arendt writes: "The recent shift of problems from the *Why* and *What* to the *How* has as its corollary that the objects of perception are processes of becoming and not things or eternal movements. . . . Particularly the natural sciences have in our time developed into specifically historical disciplines." [31] It follows that the link, which binds the humanities and natural sciences together, is history. The second law of thermodynamics contains the principle of physics which indicates the "historicity of nature." [32] The measure of thermodynamic probability—or entropy—formulated here plays an important role in the theory of information and is extremely helpful in examining social, psychological, and pedagogical processes of information. What- and Why-questions tend toward metaphysics, toward ontology; How-questions have a tendency toward technology, they point to areas of doing. "Technology may be understood as an intentional creation and application of means through which effects can be attained at will, effects which would not have occurred by themselves." [33]

[28] Th. W. Adorno, *Jargon der Eigentlichkeit. Zur deutschen Ideologie* (Frankfurt, 1964), p. 13.

[29] H. Asmussen, *Zur gegenwärtigen Lage der Ev. Kirche in Deutschland* (Berlin, 1952), p. 7. Cf. H. Asmussen, "Sprache als theologisches Problem," *Interpretation der Welt. Festschrift für R. Guardini* (Würzburg, 1965), pp. 646 ff.

[30] Th. W. Adorno, *Negative Dialektik* (Frankfurt, 1966), p. 13.

[31] H. Arendt, *Vita activa oder Vom tätigen Leben* (Stuttgart, 1960), p. 289.

[32] C. F. von Weizsäcker, *Die Geschichte der Natur* (Stuttgart, 1954), pp. 35 ff.

[33] C. F. von Weizsäcker, *Gedanken über unsere Zukunft* (Göttingen, 1966), p. 7.

There is no reason to panic, if we insist that in exactly this sense practical theology possesses a technological component. Since the church daily provokes a mass of effects, which are possible only through the creation and application of means, theology cannot get around reflecting about what these means accomplish and what they signify. It is altogether impossible, for example, to imagine the Reformation without the technique of printing —that precursor of modern mass communications. A technologically interested theology does not find it insignificant that an enormously high share of new German publications from 1518 on were Luther's own writings. Inkpot and pen, type box and printing press form the technological context for the popular theme of "Luther's hermeneutics." Contemporary practical theology is still generally working in ways which technologically date back to the times before Johannes Gutenberg's invention. There is little interest in criteria for the church's work with the mass media, the press, radio and television, not to speak of the fact that such criteria do not even exist [34]—and this when the technology of the communications media has long since totally altered the hermeneutical place of the sermon. The pulpit, also a technological medium, has slid from its central position in the medieval community into the sectarian corner of the secular-technological metropolis. "As a matter of fact, preaching has long since ceased to be regarded as a unique procedure in the secular sense, as in Reformation times. Rather it has been evicted from the midst of contemporary talk-culture by forensic and political, by academic as well as popular didactic exhortation, as, for example, in radio and television. . . . Precisely because there is an oversupply of talk, people today have become bad listeners." [35] While we agree with Trillhaas' analysis of the theory of communications, we must object to his judgment of the listener. Man in a technological age does not hear worse than his non-technological ancestor, he merely hears differently. Technology simply is not something that despicably exists side by side with man; it is above all no hermeneutic adiaphoron. Man and machine enter into a symbiosis. A man in front of a radio becomes a radio listener, and as such he acts quite differently from an abstract being "man," next to whom someone happens to have placed a talking machine. Newspaper reader, television viewer, telephone user, paperback buyer, poster viewer—all these diverse roles, which modern technological talk-culture offers to and imposes upon contemporary man, all these through their effectiveness also determine the role of the modern hearer of sermons. The doctrine of the Word of God usually does not give a hoot in what particular

[34] This gap is explored by *Medium,* a periodical for Protestant radio and television work published in Munich since 1964 and supported by people practically involved in the media. Cf. particularly A. van den Heuvel, "Ueberlegungen zum Thema: Theologie, Kommunikation und Massenmedien," *Medium* 4 (1967), 149 ff.

[35] Trillhaas, "Die wirkliche Predigt," p. 197.

technical medium the church's speaking finds a home. When it talks about new possibilities of the language about God, it means something pentecostal which cannot be done but only hoped for. So everything remains in fact as it has always been. Whatever else is being said about the technological talk-civilization is inevitably taken from bad-tempered cultural criticism: "The flood of words, the materialization of language and the substitution of pictures for language. . . . We live in an age characterized by an overflow of words and a loss of words." [36]

Practical Theology and the Empirical

As far as we know there is no study in the theory of language which holds the growing vocabulary of our contemporaries responsible for possible difficulties in understanding. George Kinsley Zipf has been the first to make a statistical study of the meaning of words in relation to the probable frequency of their use. In a law bearing his name [37] he expressed his findings that the number of diverse meanings of a word increases with the frequency of its use. Where are the linguistic criteria for the harsh theological strictures against modern information techniques, television, and opinion forming devices? What sense is there in maligning the technical media of the present without recognizing that their functioning assures and continued existence of the social structure? Scientific investigation of the media has long recognized the danger of a hypertrophy of optical and acoustic stimulation.[38] Certainly it is no longer possible to regard technology as a deficient mode of the theological. It is not at all a matter of indifference whether the most important books by Barth, Bultmann, Ebeling, Marxsen, etc. are used only by experts, or whether they can be purchased by anyone at every railroad station newstand.[39] What is the significance of preaching in an age when everything can be technically reproduced?—to modify slightly a well-known question by W. Benjamin. What changes are taking place in the church, when Barth's preaching is available on records, when other current significant radio sermons (Gollwitzer, Thielicke, etc.) can be preserved on tape by any amateur? Just as recorded music has become competition for every band director in the province, since the hearer takes his standards from the highest musical achievements, so the "canned" sermon creates an

[36] Moltmann, "Wort Gottes und Sprache," pp. 390 and 389.
[37] J. R. Pierce, *Phänomene der Kommunikation. Informationstheorie, Nachrichtenübertragung, Kybernetik* (Düsseldorf-Vienna, 1965), pp. 269 ff.
[38] C. Feldmann, *Theorie der Massenmedien. Presse, Film, Funk, Fernsehen* (Munich-Basel, 1962); G. Maletzke, *Psychologie der Massenkommunikation. Theorie und Systematik* (Hamburg, 1963); H. K. Platte, *Soziologie der Massenkommunikationsmittel. Analysen und Berichte* (Munich-Basel, 1965).
[39] Cf. H. M. Enzensberger, "Bildung als Konsumgut. Analyse der Taschenbuch-Produktion," *Einzelheiten* (Frankfurt, 1962), pp. 110 ff.

invisible effect: A pastor can no longer act as though the pulpit were standing in the center of the church. What are we to say when a congregation hears a sermon indirectly on tape rather than in face-to-face communication? This actually happened at the Ecumenical Service of 1966 in Switzerland with a sermon by the American minister Martin Luther King, Jr. How are we to deal with the events of the German Evangelical *Kirchentag*, which far beyond its actual physical presence reproduces itself in public through radio and television, the press and books? The category of the "public," which is of such fundamental importance in the Reformation theology of worship, can today be understood only if technology is included in the consideration. To do this means that the parochial realm of the church becomes problematic in its claim to represent the public realm. "We must clearly understand that our worship in the realm of the church no longer constitutes a public realm in the same sense as it . . . did in the Constantinian epoch of church history. The sermon no longer reaches the ears of those who determine the public realm, and it no longer has power to shape the public." [40] Luther's polemic against the "private mass" was a refutation of any kind of proclamation "in the corner." His understanding of the sermon implies speaking publicly, using the word "in vogue." The modern public realm [41] reveals altogether different structural elements. It is mediated technologically, that is, "made," managed, and constantly threatened with manipulation. Therefore it needs critique and control. Two prejudices currently prevent theological contact with this changed public realm: (1) As long as the doctrine of the Word of God speculatively acts as the guardian of practical theology, the technical world is either ignored or secretly relegated to the realm of the demonic by way of Heidegger's debasing rune of "Gestell." (2) The classical disciplines of practical theology, homiletics, catechetics, liturgics, etc. are incompetent to deal with substantive questions of the church's actions in an age of technological publicity. They are not only one-sidedly structured in terms of pastoral theology, but they are institutionally perceived as well. As academic disciplines the "instruction in preaching," "care of souls," etc. correspond neatly and fully to the parochial institutions of the middle-class folk church of the nineteenth century. The current problems of the church's publicity are inaccessible to the reflections of practical theology in principle as long as they are approached homiletically, since then the traditional image of preaching immediately presses to the forefront as an archetype. An analysis of the

[40] H. R. Müller-Schwefe, *Die Lehre von der Verkündigung. Homiletik* II (Hamburg, 1965), 258.
[41] J. Habermas, *Strukturwandel der Öffentlichkeit. Untersuchungen zu einer Kategorie der bürgerlichen Gesellschaft* (Neuwied, 1965); H. J. Schultz, "Die unbewältigte Öffentlichkeit der Kirche," *Jenseits des Weihrauchs, theologia publica,* 1 (Freiburg, 1966), 17 ff.

forms of the church's speaking (*Formgeschichte*), which an empirical practical theology would have to work out for its time, would assign to pulpit speaking a very specific place in the context of the church's actions. But it could do so only after it had evaluated the communicative achievements of the pulpit in comparison with other forms of contact. Catechetics as the doctrine of the church's teaching is ultimately also too hard pressed, if it is asked to relate in substantive fashion to the whole wide field of the modern science of education.[42] Conversely, theories of teaching and learning, of education and instruction reach far beyond institutionalized religious instruction and are of real concern to the whole realm of the church's actions.

Our habitual antipathy against How-questions originates in a dead or dying metaphysics which knows how to pass off its truths as content, core, and above all as problems of essence in an impenetrable depth. The traditional Aristotelian dichotomy of content and form has been replaced in the empirical fact-oriented sciences of the present with the duality of structure and function. In keeping with a contemporary theoretical approach, Georg Picht, in his "Structure and Responsibility of the Sciences in the Twentieth Century," inquires: "In place of the old basic question: 'What can we know?' we now have a new basic question: 'What can we do?' The possibility of doing is regarded as a new criterion of truth; right is what 'works,' what functions." [43] Technological intelligence then masters such possibilities of doing as plan and organization, as order and system. This does not at all mean that the whole of reality is planned or that we are establishing a dictatorship of manipulation. The concept of reality in the contemporary sciences is not deterministic-causal, but statistical (one could also say, historical). It encompasses accident and necessity, freedom and plan, the irregular and the regular. The ideal of technological intelligence is therefore no longer Laplace's demon who overlooks all realities, because he knows all causes. The logic of fact-oriented research regards plan and freedom, contingency and stringency as dialectically connected, although it does so without giving the phenomenological intuition or *Wesensschau* a serious chance anywhere.[44] The dialectic of accident and necessity is de-

[42] Cf. H. Kittel, "Der Stand der Religionspädagogik und die religionspädagogische Ausbildung," ThPr 1:3 (1966), 207 ff.

[43] G. Picht, *Der Gott der Philosophen und die Wissenschaft der Neuzeit* (Stuttgart, 1966), p. 82.

[44] K. Mannheim, *Wissenssoziologie*, K. H. Wolff, ed. (Berlin-Neuwied, 1964), p. 334: "The phenomenological school is not necessarily a Catholic philosophy (though its ancestry include Bolzano and Brentano). Yet in essential points it is exceedingly well suited to undergird anew the Catholic 'eternity-thinking' from a fresh point of view. Its radical separation between factual and essential knowledge revives and legitimizes the sharp duality between the temporal and the eternal and opens up the possibility of a content-filled metaphysics. In the phenomenological view of being there are several contents which may be taken as transtemporal." The question deserves consideration, whether Evangelical theology is not substantively closer to empirical research than phenomenology. The work

manded by human intelligence and not derived from some mysterious world spirit. This is exactly what Carl Friedrich von Weizsäcker means with his sentence: "But we must plan the area in which freedom is possible." [45] Our thesis is as follows: Practical theology is the place where the church's actions are reflected under the aspects of plan and freedom, organization and improvisation, reality and possibility. This takes place by generally abstaining from questions of essence [46] and by paying close attention to the guiding motifs of theory and practice. These we must now consider in detail.

Manfred Mezger rightly contends that "the commonly held notion of the 'practical' (a few practical exercises, 'how it's done') is no good and does a lot of harm." [47] Those who busily add up their experiences are not yet empirical in the scientific sense; and Kant already has charged the collector of naked facts with having "delusions of wisdom together with the eyesight of a mole." [48] Just as we cannot call the mere observation of practice empirical, so theory must not be confused with the attempt to reproduce any group of facts photographically. Adorno writes: "The object of theory is not something immediately given whose imprint it can carry home; perception, unlike the FBI, does not possess an album of its objects." [49] Theory is neither reproduction nor reflex, it is rather a synthetic achievement between experience and intelligence. For fact-oriented research (*Tatsachenwissenschaft*) there is then no "pure experience," but only experience in the light of theory. The latter however transcends all experiences in order to interpret them properly. Theory is an expression of conscious and intended abstraction. Talcott Parsons says: "Theory is a body of interrelated generalized propositions about empirical phenomena within a frame of reference." [50] The empirical facts and their theoretical frames of reference are reciprocally interconnected. Neither facts nor theories exist independently of each other "in-themselves." They alternately imply and change each other. The proper evidence for an empirical fact is therefore not something natural, naïve and

---

of K. Schwarzwäller, *Theologie der Phänomenologie. Erwägungen zur Methodik theologischen Verstehens* (Munich, 1966), is unfortunately uninformed, as far as the theory of science is concerned.

[45] C. F. von Weizsäcker, *Gedanken über unsere Zukunft*, p. 20.

[46] The Word-of-God theology insists on "essence." Thus, H.-R. Müller-Schwefe for example begins his *Homiletik* I (Hamburg, 1961), 19, with the question of the "essence of language," and his *Homiletik* II, 15, with the question of the "essence of proclamation."

[47] M. Mezger, "Praktische Theologie—Zugang zu ihrem Studium I," ThPr 1:2 (1966), 115.

[48] Immanuel Kant, "Über den Gemeinspruch: Das mag in der Theorie richtig sein, taugt aber nicht für die Praxis" (1793), *Kleine Schriften zur Geschichtsphilosophie, Ethik und Politik*, K. Vorländer, ed. (Hamburg, 1959), p. 71.

[49] Adorno, *Dialektik*, p. 204.

[50] T. Parsons, "Culture and the Social System," in *Theory of Sociology-Foundations of Modern Sociological Theory* II, T. Parsons, E. Schils, K. Naegele, J. Pitts, eds. (New York, 1962, 2nd ed.), 695.

accessible to everyone, but it is "an evidence aimed at artificially," as Stephan Strasser has clearly put it.[51] The empirical fact is founded upon a methodological idea. The logician Karl R. Popper defines this precisely: "The empirical sciences are theoretical systems. . . . Theory is the net we cast out to capture 'the world,'—in order to rationalize it, to explain and to dominate it. We are always trying to make the mesh of the net still finer." [52] The figure of speech used by Popper is symptomatic. Modern scientific logic does not regard reality as a ready-built home, where one has only to look for the key, to file it and to use it, and the doors of any room will open. The world is more like an ocean, where at every moment every wave changes all; and science is like a boat whose pilots orient themselves with maps which they did not find in the water but "invented" through disciplined thinking about their experiences. Popper emphatically cites a letter from Albert Einstein in which the latter tells he "is thinking that theory cannot be fabricated from the results of observation, but can only be invented." [53]

As a matter of fact, there is no fundamental difference between the logic of the natural sciences and that of other fact-oriented research (*Tatsachenforschung*). C. F. von Weizsäcker specifically regards it as one of the main weaknesses of Aristotle that he was too naïvely empirical, too realistic in his observation of nature. "Galileo took a giant step when he dared to describe the world as we do not experience it. He formulated laws which—in the form in which he expressed them—could never hold in our actual experience and which therefore can never be confirmed by any single observation." [54] And Ralf Dahrendorf writes regarding the theoretical construction of the *homo sociologicus:* "In this sense, the less realistic a theory is, that is, the more stylized, definite and unambiguous its assumptions are, the better it is." [55]

At this point let us inject the problem of practical theology. We have insisted that practical theology turn toward fact-oriented research; and this subordinates it to the guiding motifs of theory and practice. Practice, toward which practical theology is directed, then is not something simply given, but must be established through methodological inquiry. The frame of reference of methodological questions in regard to the church's actions yields the research area of practical theology. The widely accepted proposition that practical theology is the theory of the church's practice is correct only if we make the prior assumption that the various facts, which

<hr/>

[51] St. Strasser, *Phänomenologie und Erfahrungswissenschaft vom Menschen. Grundgedanken zu einem neuen Ideal der Wissenschaftlichkeit* (Berlin, 1964), p. 116.

[52] K. R. Popper, *Logik der Forschung* (Tübingen, 1966), p. 31.

[53] *Ibid.,* p. 413.

[54] C. F. von Weizsäcker, *Die Tragweite der Wissenschaft* I (Stuttgart, 1966), 107.

[55] R. Dahrendorf, "Soziologie," in *Wege zur pädagogischen Anthropologie,* A. Flitner, ed. (Heidelberg, 1963), p. 115.

constitute ecclesiastical practice, are not statically given, but have been artificially evoked by methodological inquiry. Practical theology, too, cannot fabricate its theories from the results of observation, but must invent them. What Heinrich Roth says of the turn toward realism in pedagogy is analogically applicable to practical theology as well: "Empirical research does not imply an acknowledgment of the normative power of the factual, an acquiescence in the real. On the contrary, it means challenging the presumed facts, the seemingly immutable given, with productive inquiry developed by the pedagogic idea, so that still hidden pedagogic possibilities may be revealed. Research is precisely openness for new experiences, a questioning of mere opinions and presumed facts." [56] It does seem that the relationship of theology to the realm of practice is as disoriented as that of pedagogy. In both, the view is obscured by speculative argumentation, by essentialistic value concepts which are derived independently from concrete references. Unless empirical research is granted voice and vote, the pedagogical concept of education is as empty of content as the theological concept of proclamation. Theological hermeneutic is in no position to change this, even if it expressly presents itself as doctrine of the Word of God.[57] H. Roth has requested that in pedagogy the hermeneutic of the historical texts be supplemented with a hermeneutic of the pedagogical field.[58] This is our key point: Practical theology as an academic discipline can fulfill its task only if it succeeds in working out a heremeneutic of the church's actions through thorough field research to complement the hermeneutic of the biblical texts. We are therefore placing side by side with the hermeneutic of the Word of God a practical hermeneutic of human words.

An Action-Science

Practical theology is neither a conservative justification of existing conditions in the church, nor is it a spiritual source of permanent reformation. Rather, its guiding motifs of theory and practice involve practical theology in the dialectic of plan and freedom, order and surprise, organization and decision. H. Schelsky has grouped disciplines such as sociology, law, psychology, and pedagogy, which in contrast with the historical, cultural disciplines are concerned with social action, into a class of social action disciplines (*soziale Handlungswissenschaften*). They all possess "this basic, direct reference to

[56] H. Roth, "Die realistische Wendung in der pädagogischen Forschung," in *Erziehungswissenschaft und Erziehungswirklichkeit,* H. Röhrs, ed. (Frankfurt, 1964), p. 184.
[57] G. Ebeling, "Wort Gottes und Hermeneutik," in *Die neue Hermeneutik* II, J. M. Robinson and J. B. Cobb, eds. (Zürich, 1965), 134.
[58] H. Roth, *Pädogogische Anthropologie* I (Hannover, 1966), 94.

current action." [59] In his paper on the Reform of the Study of Practical Theology,[60] presented at the Second International Conference on Practical Theology at Jena, also Gerhard Krause commendably dealt with the present discussions in the theory of science and defined practical theology as the "science of the church's action." This has opened a door which we would decidedly like to enter. The distinguishing mark of the modern action-sciences is theory which, as an open system of cognition, is constantly altered by new empirical evidence. Theory is not content with making explicit what anyone can see in any case. It claims to be fruitful, i.e., to prove itself in the dialectic of planning and deciding. Here we are reminded of A. Comte: "*voire pour prévoir pour prévenir.*" Modern theory does not emancipate itself from practice; it does not leave the action-related areas to their own rules in order freely to pay homage to some sort of vain scientific ideal unencumbered by any purpose and endowed with pseudo-sovereignty. The classical contradiction in the theory of science between purpose-free education and pragmatic training is out of date, if we recognize that the dialectical relation between theory and practice points to a new understanding which bases practice on theory and relates theory to practice. In this sense, Jürgen Habermas challenges dialectical theory "to rediscover the socially given as that which is self-made" and to proceed "as if that which comes to us as object of our experience were a product of our own practice." [61] The cognitive interest of this theory is both critical and purposive. It calls for an awareness, which is able to see through the normative powers of the factual and can "neutralize [them] by determined negation," which in turn means that practice is based on critique. Even under the guidance of such a theoretical awareness, Habermas feels, "practice still could not possibly accomplish anything which does not already hold us in its grip as our own doing; but it would at least know this and could therefore guard against being trapped in unfreedom by our freedom yet unaware of itself." [62] In his work, Habermas has thoroughly analyzed the position of theory as a problem of technological intelligence which must delineate its areas of freedom. A practical theology, which shuns the tasks of rationalization, which resists the theologically relevant powers-that-be with speculative prudery, would in the long run only deliver itself blindly to any kind of domination and would betray the church's actions to the automatisms of

[59] Schelsky, *Einsamkeit und Freiheit*, p. 283. [*Translator's note:* I have rendered the term "Handlungswissenschaft" as "action-science" rather than using the more common—and more loaded—term "behavorial science." The reason will hopefully be apparent from the context.]

[60] ZThK 64 (1967), 474 ff., esp. 484.

[61] J. Habermas, "Über das Verhältnis von Politik und Moral," in *Das Problem der Ordnung* (*Sechster Deutscher Kongress für Philosophie,* Munich, 1960), H. Kuhn, F. Wiedmann, eds. (Meisenheim, 1962), p. 115.

[62] Habermas, *ibid.*, p. 115.

61

totalitarian coercion. "The argument no longer holds that the whole cannot be done because we can never know it objectively; for we start doing it daily, albeit without knowing it, but not unawares, rather—in contrast with earlier epochs—precisely with full scientific awareness. Scientifically guided practice yields more of the planned than its input of plans. The un-identified surplus is an unconscious element in scientific awareness which keeps the latter from becoming awareness of itself." [63] This strikingly turns upside down the idealistic relationship between theory and practice. Hegel's heraldic animal of theory, the owl of Minerva, now no longer flies away only at dusk, when practice is off the job, so that our insights invariably arrive too late, but it takes to the air before sunrise, surveys the fields of action and joins in every activity with the critical analysis of a technically equipped intelligence. In contemporary theology awareness is still widely lagging behind. Werner Jetter writes: "Theology is not creative, but re-flective. Basically, it does not produce new epochs, not even in its reforma-tory breakthroughs. Rather it conceptualizes them in the process of formulat-ing, translating and interpreting what God himself has previously typed on the secular stencils of world history." [64] What is here dogmatically pre-supposed is precisely what needs to be critically examined: Is it really God who types the stencils, or might it not be some powerful institution, a blind habit, or a clever government cunningly hiding its totalitarian traits behind the totality of God? Under the guiding motifs of theory and practice practical theology ceases to be merely reflective. It is critically oriented when it focuses on tradition; it is empirically oriented when it analyzes the complexes of contemporary action; it plans prospectively when it considers the future.

The natural and behavioral sciences have long confronted the fact that the results of their theoretical research will sooner or later be translated into practice. A lack of awareness here can only lead to disastrous conse-quences. G. Picht warns: "Unless theory understands itself as radical prac-tice, practice of a completely different sort, namely of political origin, will only too easily be able to take over science and will impose laws upon it which are neither scientifically nor morally defensible.[65] Picht demands that we "develop a theory of the consequences of science, which itself would then become the guideline for that kind of practice which alone can master

[63] *Ibid.*, p. 114.

[64] W. Jetter, "Der Pluralismus in der Kirche—Reaktion oder Konzeption?" ThPr I:1 (1966), 45. Jetter has recently corrected his position: "The bottlenecks in the service of the church have become so noticeable, that we must expect pace-making services from practical theology and not merely marginal notes." "Die Praktische Theologie," ZThK 64 (1967), 470. This essay has basically a different starting point than our discussion, but many goals are similar.

[65] G. Picht, *Die Verantwortung des Geistes. Pädagogische und politische Schriften* (Freiburg, 1965), p. 145.

the consequences of science. . . . Into this large context belongs also—and in a central place—the problem of translating the insights of science into the process of forming the future citizens of a scientific world." [66] Even those who are in sympathy with practical theology cannot really claim that it has thoroughly concerned itself with the consequences of theological research. The results of theological research rather have reached the public quite accidentally and partly by strange circuitous routes. Thus, Dorothee Sölle was able to note quite correctly in reference to Bishop Robinson's well-known book: "It is not without irony that German theology had to go to England and be translated there into clear and everywhere comprehensible language, so that now it may possibly have a chance here [in Germany] too." [67] And Ernst Käsemann declares in regard to the polemic about scriptural interpretation: "It cannot be denied that in the past and present theology has generally failed pedagogically, although we may be able to explain it and to show that for the most part this was unavoidable." [68] A practical theology, which is aware of the contemporary relationship between theory and practice, here feels called to its task. It has to understand that there are no other forms of behavior open to church and Christianity than those which our scientific civilization offers elsewhere. There scientific theory is more and more taking the place of natural, immediate experiences. Theory discloses reality for us in the first place, guides its development as far as this can be done and keeps it open for necessary changes. So science becomes, as Joachim Ritter writes, "the organ of experience and of actualization in a world where for the first time in history we depend on science even in the elementary areas." [69] We can currently study the theological relevance of these sentences in the polemic about the Bible in our churches up and down our country. At a time when contemplative meditation is crowded out by a desire for conceptual awareness,[70] the call for scientific information sounds loud and clear. It is no accident that the conference programs of the Evangelical Academies and the *Kirchentage* cluster in this area. Nor is the constant participation of scientific resource persons in

[66] *Ibid.*, pp. 144-45.

[67] D. Sölle, "Aufklärung über den Glauben," in *Diskussion zu Bischof Robinsons Gott ist anders*, H. W. Augustin, ed. (Munich, 1964), p. 164.

[68] E. Käsemann, "Zum gegenwärtigen Streit um die Schriftauslegung," *Exegetische Versuche und Besinnungen* II (Göttingen, 1964), 281.

[69] J. Ritter, "Die Aufgabe der Geisteswissenschaften in der modernen Gesellschaft," *Jahresschrift der Gesellschaft zur Förderung der Westfälischen Wilhelms-Universität zu Münster* (Münster, 1961), p. 39.

[70] Symptomatic is a sentence by G. Otto from his introduction to the reader in contemporary Protestant theology, "Glauben heute," *Stundenbuch* 48 (Hamburg, 1965), 12, a book which Otto edited: "The function, formerly handled by books on meditation, must now be taken over by expository works designed to clarify the concepts presented to us by contemporary theology."

events of this kind unintentional.[71] In view of these changed realities, a practical theology which unperturbedly continues to spell out homiletics, liturgics, and catechetics does seem strangely absentminded. It should be our task to support these significant changes in the church's actions critically as a product of our own theological practice. For the new situation gives rise to new dangers. On the one hand, an ideology of naïve faith in science[72] brings with it its own theological variants; on the other, the disciplines of theology, just like the other sciences, tend to become the domain of specialized research with its ever-increasing demands. "Those who are not engaged [in specialized research], even the well educated, then are no longer in the role of the amateur who complements the professional, but they take on the role of the layman who only watches from outside." Hans Freyer[73] speaks of a second-hand knowing and thinking, of a "consumer's stance," "a piece of the general culture of consumption." What does it mean theologically, when the church's laity—and beyond that the scientifically educated practitioner, pastor, teacher, etc., as well—is squeezed and pushed into behaving like a consumer, into second-hand thinking? How do we understand a Christian existence which is molded in its own way by the cultural norms of consumer orientation? What consequences arise, when theological knowledge increases each year by a calculable ratio, doubles x-yearly, and multiples itself in a manner analogous to that of the other sciences? What is the significance of theological study, whose attained knowledge, measured in terms of the progress of research, can be "consumed" in five to ten years of practice? For this phenomenon there is at present scarcely an insight, rarely a diagnosis, and hardly a therapy. If practical theology persists in neglecting the problem of theory and practice methodologically, it may well be that the figure of the scribe will rise up again in dual awfulness: in a speculating Bible specialist who doesn't miss a chance to appeal to the Word of God, and in a theologically uninformed congregation who in dull ignorance falls for every ideological seduction.

We would thoroughly misunderstand practical theology as the church's action-science, if we tried to use it directly in the service of the pastoral and administrative offices of the church as a kind of auxiliary science. If we take our task on commission by the church's institutions, the whole enterprise would be corrupted before the problems of theory and practice have a chance to surface. The constantly debated question, whether prac-

---

[71] At the 1965 Cologne *Kirchentag*, 22 of 42 speakers were professors and university instructors. Cf. *Erlebter Kirchentag Köln 1965* (Stuttgart-Berlin, 1965), pp. 281 ff.

[72] Cf. von Weizsäcker, *Die Tragweite der Wissenschaft* I, 3 ff. The problem is theologically considered by H. Kittel, "Wissenschaft in der Schule?" in *Ein anderes Evangelium? Wissenschaftliche Theologie und Christliche Gemeinde*, K. Aland, ed. (Witten, 1967), pp. 148 ff.

[73] H. Freyer, "Die Wissenschaft des 20. Jahrhunderts und die Idee der humanistischen Bildung," *Erkenntnis und Verantwortung, Litt Festschrift* (Düsseldorf, 1960), p. 149.

tical theology belongs to the academic program of the university or would be better taken care of in the church's own educational institutions, reveals a dangerous ignorance of the contemporary theory-practice problem. Modern fact-oriented research which has so thoroughly altered the classical distinctions up to and including the thesis of theory as radical practice—modern fact-oriented research specifically insists on the strict separation of analysis and decision, of theoretical awareness and pragmatic action. Of course, one will have to correct Max Weber's conception of truth, which distinguished in principle between the scientific teaching of what *can* be and what *should* be.[74] The theoretical awareness of research is bracketing practice, moving ahead of it through planning, walking aside it in critique, and following after in reflection. But in all this it categorically refuses to equate theory and practice. Adorno talks about this as "a violent act of equalizing" which must be blamed on an undialectic desire for identity. "The demand for an identity of practice and theory has inexorably reduced the latter to servitude; it has destroyed the very thing that theory was supposed to contribute to that unity. The practical mark of approval which is being required of all theory has become a stamp of censorship. Since however in the famed unity of theory and practice the former lost out, the latter also lost its conceptual identity and became part of the very politics beyond which it was supposed to have led us. Practice was handed over to power. Liquidating theory through dogmatization and suppression of thought contributed to bad practice. It is in the interest of practice itself that theory should regain its autonomy."[75] These sentences should be memorized by all who would like to equate practical theology with theological-ecclesiastical practice. It should be in their own very specific interest to insist that practical theology produce fruitful theories. But these can be produced only if an antagonistic autonomy is assured. Habermas speaks of the dual task of sociology, a critical and a conservative one. Practical theology also is both, applied to the church: the science of opposition and the science of stabilization.[76]

The most difficult problems facing the theory of science today in regard to the relationship of theory and practice are posed by the so-called "big science," the project sciences.[77] These are introducing a completely new type of science. They are at the same time scientifically, politically, and eco-

[74] Cf. L. Raiser, *Wissenschaft als Beruf. Neu erörtert* (Stuttgart, 1964); H. Lübbe, "Die Freiheit der Theorie. Max Weber über Wissenschaft als Beruf," *Archiv für Rechts- und Sozialphilosophie* XLVIII (1962), 343 ff.

[75] Adorno, *Negative Dialektik*, pp. 144-45.

[76] J. Habermas, "Kritische und konservative Aufgaben der Soziologie," *Theorie und Praxis. Sozialpsychologische Studien* (Neuwied, 1963), p. 228.

[77] W. Häfele, "Die Projektwissenschaften," *Radius*, 3 (1965), 3 ff.; also, Häfele, "Geplante Zukunft. Der Beitrag der Wissenschaft zum Frieden," *Der Frieden ist unter uns* (Stuttgart, 1967), pp. 15 ff. G. Picht also deals with "big science" in *Der Gott der Philosophen*, pp. 87 ff.

nomically conditioned. Their work is supported by scientific institutions, political governments, and industry. Wolf Häfele places the project sciences side by side with basic research in the old style, because they do not merely aim at theoretical knowledge but, beyond that, at its technical application on which, at least in part, the very survival of a community may depend. The project sciences are creating an artificial nature in the shape of physical energy, but also in the form of pedagogically relevant systems (e.g., educational programs). This enterprise, the artificial conditioning of human learning, has a direct bearing on the specific interests of practical theology. With some problems of church action it will no longer be possible to distribute responsibility individually between theoretical intelligence on the one hand and practical decision on the other. There will have to be a corporate collaboration between representatives of scientific theology and church administration. "It seems that the extraordinarily complex admixture of scientific initiative, problem identification, political clarification, re-examination of the problem and its final solution, constitutes a complicated process of reiteration in which a considerable exchange of ideas between scientists, politicians, and business leaders is prerequisite for the final solution of the problem. As every student of mathematics knows, such a process of reiteration, in the course of the reiterative cycles, leads to constant changes in the starting position of all participants, the scientists and the politicians. It follows that the responsibility clearly does not rest with the individual partner in the reiterative process alone, such as the scientist or the politician. There is a joint responsibility, an admixture." [78]

The discovery of the controlled feedback loop in cybernetics most clearly demonstrates the close proximity between modern scientific theory and technology. Thinking in terms of feedback loops has made its appearance even in areas where until now purpose-free research had been the order of the day. What does this mean for the relationship between theory and practice? In traditional concepts, the *homo sapiens* and the *homo faber* irreconcilably oppose each other. Goethe knew of this antagonism better than almost anyone and made it a frequent topic of his aphorisms in *Maximen und Reflexionen*. What he had sensed and felt has probably been fruitfully reconsidered only in the most recent discussions. "Theory and experience (phenomenon) stand opposed in constant conflict. Every attempt to unify them through reflection is an illusion; they can be united only through action." [79] The irreconcilable opposition between thought and action is a serious matter. In the last analysis it gives our world the quality of a stage set for tragedy, where theoreticians make things ineffectively abstract (*kopfrecht*), and practitioners make them effectively handy (*handrecht*).[80] But the tragic law applies to both: "Those

[78] Häfele, "Die Projektwissenschaften," p. 13.
[79] Goethe, "Maximen und Reflexionen," Hamburg Edition XII: 497.
[80] *Ibid.*, No. 234.

who act are always without conscience; there is no one with a conscience except the man who contemplates." [81] What Goethe is describing here has become a vexing problem in the twentieth century as the Robert Oppenheimer syndrome—and not only for the physicist. Theory, which provides the rationale for practice, can no longer exempt itself from its consequences. For the theologian this means: He can no longer dogmatically, exegetically, or in some other way seek triumphs as the *homo (in theologia) sapiens* while the *homo (in ecclesia) faber*, more or less "unconscionably," is running the empirical church into the ground. The marks left by the *Kirchenkampf* here serve as an immediate, deterrent object lesson. Researchers today generally agree that Protestant Christianity had been unprepared for this kind of conflict situation and its concomitant diverse individual questions (dictatorship, the ideology of fatherland, relationship to Israel). What consequences has theology after 1945 drawn from these experiences? [82] Has practical theology specifically made an attempt to work out a theoretical plan[83] by analyzing conflict-prone factors so that we are prepared for similar dangers? In opposition to church politics and church movements, Karl Barth in those days proclaimed, from the standpoint of the Word-words dialectic, a theological existence which in the face of temptation called for a turn to essentials and for renewed certainty. The constructive contribution of the theological *homo sapiens* consisted in "doing theology, and only theology, in a slightly heightened tone but without direct references." [84] Barth categorically refused to say anything "about the situation." We do not intend here to analyze the position taken by a great theologian in the context of church history. Rather we are asking, how are we to evaluate Barth's action in regard to the relationship between theory and practice? May it be considered as representative of comparable situations? We are looking for the theoretical link between the teacher of church dogmatics and the author of the numerous political paraeneses. The position proposed by Barth for a scientific theologian, that of the lonely "bird perched on the roof, that is, on the earth but under an open, wide and absolutely open sky," [85] that position poses a problem, when we are thinking cybernetically in terms of controlled feedback. For the bird's-eye view has always been the optics of the *homo sapiens* who, on account of his desperate observations and occasionally with a loud warning cry, is trying to deter the *homo faber* from

[81] *Ibid.*, No. 251.

[82] Cf. the research of E. Wolf, esp. *Kirche im Widerstand? Protestantische Opposition in der Klammer der Zweireichelehre* (Munich, 1965).

[83] K. Lüthi asks, "What is the fundamental meaning for faith, for theology, for ethics, of Hiroshima (what of Auschwitz, etc.)?" K. Lüthi, "Liebe 1957—Eine theologische Interpretation des Filmtextes 'Hiroshima mon amour,'" *Freude am Evangelium—Festschrift für A. de Quervain* (1966), p. 70.

[84] K. Barth, *Theologische Existenz heute* (Munich, 1933), p. 3.

[85] *Ibid.*, p. 40.

his actions—generally without success, as we know. For the cybernetician the problem is technical. The duality of the *homo sapiens* and the *homo faber* appears to him like a moving machine without a steering mechanism. He therefore complements the aspects of theoretical research and practical action with a third one: the technical aspect of control and steering. So the *homo sapiens*, who thinks things abstractly, and the *homo faber*, who practices them handily, are joined by the *homo ludens*, who mediates between thought and action by steering and controlling. The concept of game playing may be misunderstood. We don't mean the poker type who unscrupulously bets all on one card to reach his goal. The aspect of game-theory rather describes the strategist who approaches reality with models. The concept of model serves technically to reconnect practice with theory. The logic of fact-oriented research does not by accident compel us to think in terms of models. "The *homo ludens* here is not a sideline of human activity, but an essential link in a chain of reconnections. The *homo sapiens* does not gain knowledge from his environment to construct from it motives, orders, directives, etc. for the *homo faber*, but initially he does so only to perfect his inner model of the outside world. With this inner model he 'plays through' the future situations of the outside world in model form. This 'playing through' of a situation in model form may be a mental process, it can however also be done with material models." [86] Our thinking in terms of controlled feedback loops has taught us to arrange our dealings with a manifold reality in such a way that model actions may be conceived and constructed which preplay the actual actions themselves so that we can get them under control. Georg Klaus, following the work of Karl Steinbuch, has most thoroughly dealt with the problem of theory and practice in cybernetic terms. He himself opens the way to theology for us: "Such models are products of the activity of the *homo ludens*. Even Luther's ninety-five theses developed a model, namely a theological model. The effect of this model on Luther's times was tremendous, yet Luther's theological model of being has never become a social reality. The same may be said of many another social utopia." [87] Under the guidance of cybernetic thinking practical theology then does not directly refer the actions of the ecclesiastical *homo faber* back to the reflections of the *homo sapiens*, but it interrupts the old cycle of reconnections by interposing the theological *homo ludens*. Specifically he carries on the business of practical theology; he does this by anticipating the situations and actions of the church's practice in model form for the purpose of gaining critical and

[86] G. Klaus, *Kybernetik und Erkenntnistheorie* (Berlin, 1966), p. 94. Cf. also K. Steinbuch, *Automat und Mensch. Kybernetische Tatsachen und Hypothesen* (Berlin-Heidelberg, 1965), and *Die informierte Gesellschaft. Geschichte und Zukunft der Nachrichtentechnik* (Stuttgart, 1966).
[87] Klaus, *Kybernetik und Erkenntnistheorie*, pp. 99-100.

a) Old Position

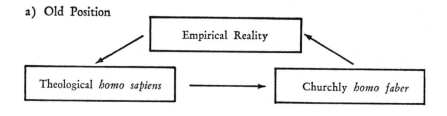

b) New Position

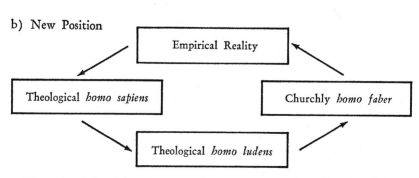

guiding foresight. The diagram above compares the old and the new positions of practical theology.[88]

This diagram easily leads us to the contention that a practical theology, which is reorienting itself cybernetically with a view to the guiding motifs of theory and practice, does in fact thoroughly alter its time aspect. It ceases to be primarily re-flection (*Nach-denken*) and becomes expressly pre-science (*Vor-sicht*). We can say with Steinbuch: "The critical view then orients itself less by the past and more by the future. . . . Its basic principle will be: The future has priority over the past!"[89] Technical cybernetics recognizes the specific superiority of the human species in man's ability to anticipate future world- and action-situations.[90] Thus Barth's theological existence would have to abandon its bird's-eye perspective from the rooftop and to exchange it for operating with strategic game models whenever it understands itself in the sense of practical theology. The dichotomy between theological words "about the substance" and church polity decisions "about the situation" can henceforth be no more permissible than a separation between content and form. Cybernetics replaces ontological metaphysics with a sign theory in which the categories of structure and function are considered as methodologically different aspects of one and the same subject matter. With the question of structure we examine the type of order prevailing in

[88] Cf. *ibid.*, p. 93. The Viennese cardinal F. König has designed a progressive program of practical theology, for which there is nothing comparable in the Protestant realm, in an article entitled "Kirche und Kommunikation," *Neues Forum* 167/168 (1967), 813 ff.

[89] K. Steinbuch, *Die informierte Gesellschaft*, p. 338.

[90] Cf. Steinbuch, *Automat und Mensch*, p. 270.

a given subject matter, with the question of function its ability to produce results. Structure determines x in view of that which is being effected; function determines x in view of what effects are being caused.

With these considerations we find ourselves in the very midst of clarifying the model concept.[91] Here it is important to note: (1) Models are always subjective; i.e., they are representations of something with which they can never be identical. (2) No model represents the original *in toto*, but each concentrates only on individual traits. (3) Models follow the purposes for which they have been designed; models can represent the form of the original (e.g., toy trains); they can agree in behavior (e.g., an object in a wind tunnel); they can be made of like material. The timetable at the train station, for example, is a model of the time function of the railroad and not interested in the railroad's structure and material. For the psychologist, white mice may become models for certain learning functions of the organism (e.g., trial and error). Such functions can be imitated with machines. Model thinking never develops ontological theories which seek to grasp reality "in itself" with ontic declarations. Rather, it limits itself to methodologically conceived questions that fit into a heuristically responsible frame of reference of possible answers. The question we must ask above all is the one concerning facts which might render false the theories we have developed. In the words of K. Popper, "The rejection of theories [is] the vehicle of scientific progress." [92] We note in passing: Theories and models are not identical. Theory is in the grasp of the *homo sapiens*; the model is the strategic construction of the *homo ludens*. Both must constantly be tested by reality.

Now, in our view, Barth's doctrine of the Word of God is a dogmatic theory, which the practical theologian must test to determine whether it is usable as a model in the church's action-science. However, since this theory cannot be used to anticipate in model form either social situations or language behavior with a view to their possible functioning, we feel compelled to vote against its acceptance. Contemporary practical theology is still far from being able to present models of church action in proper form. The classical disciplines, in this question too, are forcing upon us a chronic shortsightedness. The center of gravity in the church's acting has long ago ceased to lie in the sermon, in education, or pastoral care, although these continue to receive the lion's share of theological attention. If with Hans Jürgen Schultz we consider the church "a function of communication," [93]

[91] Several articles in the periodical *Studium Generale,* 18 (1965), are devoted to the model concept in the theory of science; cf. esp. H. Stachowiak, "Gedanken zur allgemeinen Theorie der Modelle," *Studium Generale,* 18 (1965), No. 7, pp. 432 ff.

[92] K. Popper, *Falsche Propheten. Hegel, Marx und die Folgen* (Berlin, 1958), p. 321.

[93] H. J. Schultz, *Konversion zur Welt. Gesichtspunkte für die Kirche von morgen. Stundenbuch* 42 (Hamburg, 1964), 77.

then it must find a theological relationship to its own effects.[94] With help from the concept of controlled feedback we are able to construct strategically relevant models for this. In conclusion we would like to attempt discussing this idea with an example. We are purposely selecting the problem of the church's language, that is, the area where we have to seek and to walk the road from the Word to the words.

A Model

The predominant doctrine of the Word of God has prevented the development of a proper doctrine of the words in modern theology. The papers read at the 1958 *Theologentag* in Berlin were sidestepping the problem of language both dogmatically and speculatively. An exception was the only non-theologian among the speakers, Karl Löwith. Our criticism is confirmed by James Barr, who recently sharply attacked the way German theologians deal with language, without the slightest awareness of linguistics.[95] Although language is at the center of attention in the present hermeneutical discussions, the basic motifs of *Sprachereignis* (language event, E. Fuchs) or *Wortgeschehen* (word event, G. Ebeling) do not get us any further, least of all to an action-science of the church. "In one way or another it is therefore necessary to watch carefully that theological hermeneutics, which operates mostly outside linguistics in the area of interpreting the Bible as God's Word or in communicating the gospel to modern man, does not exert an unfortunate and often unintended influence on the evaluation of the specifically linguistic material." [96] We intend to go still a step further than Barr and submit that without linguistic efforts the communication of the gospel to modern man cannot possibly succeed. Just as an exegete cannot get along without knowledge of philological methods, unless he wants to be considered a dilettante, so practical theology is unthinkable apart from linguistic methods. What good does it do, when M. Mezger appeals to the minister that he should let no one surpass him in "his trust in the Word" (to borrow a phrase of Albrecht Goes)? [97] Whom does it help, when Ebeling looks down on general language theory and tries "to determine the fundamental human situation from the essence of language," which then—what happy circumstance—has so very much in common with the situation intended by the word "God"? [98] The more theology considers itself capable of the irrational enterprise of reserving for the church's language

[94] Cf. Schultz, *Öffentlichkeit*, pp. 17-18.
[95] J. Barr, *Bibelexegese und moderne Semantik. Theologische und linguistische Methode in der Bibelwissenschaft* (Munich, 1965), p. 274.
[96] *Ibid.*, p. 276.
[97] Mezger, "Die Amtshandlungen der Kirche als Verkündigung," p. 62.
[98] G. Ebeling, *Gott und Wort* (Tübingen, 1966), pp. 52-53.

about God a language concept endowed with special blessings, the more speechless and poor in expression the church's practice is bound to become. There is nothing divine or magical behind words like "God," "resurrection," etc. They are not archetypes whose essence an "intuitive view" may bring to light. "Words, as everyone now knows, 'mean' nothing by themselves, although the belief that they did . . . was once equally universal. It is only when a thinker makes use of them that they stand for anything, or, in one sense, having 'meaning.' They are instruments." [99] C. K. Ogden and I. A. Richards, who wrote this sentence in their much reprinted classic of modern language science,[100] were not even mentioned in the hermeneutical discussions about the problem of "meaning." Practical theology as an empirical action-science dismisses metaphysics from language theory as well and replaces ontological speculation about being with the theory of language signs. Ontology is being pushed out by semantics. The question of the "essence" of language has been rendered obsolete by the problem of "how does language work?" The church's action must be understood and analyzed rigorously as "linguistic behavior," as "significant behavior."

With this as our goal we leave the Word and move closer to the words, to sentences, and other empirical language forms. To indulge in linguistic overconfidence here would, however, also be missing the boat. Everyone who has dealt with the complex of "the power of words" has every reason to mistrust language. "Far removed from being a guide to truth, [language] rather engulfs man in an almost inescapable web of difficulties and errors. . . . People falsely believe that their reason governs their words, when in fact language has power over their thinking. But philosophical critique has the task and the ability to uncover these influences and to render them harmless." [101] Ernst Topitsch designates as empty those language formulations which, without any noticeable subject matter, merely pretend to contain a constancy of highest principles in order to produce an emotional effect and to yield useful results in the guidance of men.[102] It is the task of the be-

[99] C. K. Ogden and I. A. Richards, *The Meaning of Meaning. A Study of the Influence of Language upon Thought and of the Science of Symbolism.* 10th ed. (London, 1960), pp. 9-10.

[100] The literature is predominantly Anglo-American. We note selectively: W. L. Anderson and N. C. Stageberg, *Introductory Readings on Language* (New York, 1966); A. Gardiner, *The Theory of Speech and Language* (Oxford, 1951); S. Chase, *Die Macht des Wortes. Das Buch von der Kommunikation* (Munich, 1955); R. H. Robins, *General Linguistics. An Introductory Survey* (London, 1965); A. Schaff, *Einführung in die Semantik,* G. Klaus, ed. (Berlin, 1966); S. Ullmann, *The Principles of Semantics* (Glasgow-Oxford, 1957); G. Klaus, *Die Macht des Wortes* (Berlin, 1965).

[101] E. Topitsch in the introduction to T. D. Weldon, *Kritik der politischen Sprache. Vom Sinn politischer Begriffe* (Neuwied, 1962), p. 17.

[102] E. Topitsch, "Über Leerformeln. Zur Pragmatik des Sprachgebrauches in Philosophie und politischer Theorie," in *Probleme der Wissenschaftstheorie. Festschrift für V. Kraft,* E. Topitsch, ed. (Vienna, 1960), pp. 233 ff. Cf. also E. Topitsch, *Sozialphilosophie zwischen Ideologie und Wissenschaft* (Neuwied, 1961).

havioral sciences to confront such pseudo-declarations with the empirical facts and to unmask them. Practical theology must constantly examine the language of the church for empty formulas. But this is impossible without language theory, linguistics, and semantics.

Among the sins of omission of contemporary practical theology, which we must accuse without leniency and extenuation, is above all its lack of interest in the secular talk-civilization. The experiences of the sermon-church with Nazism should really have been sufficient to make manifest the terrible power and impotence of which human words are capable. Every action of the regime was introduced by a declaration; the word reliably preceded every deed and misdeed. A doctrine of preaching for the "servant of the Word" is a foolhardy charade when it fails to notice how callously effective the dictators of words are in manipulating their hearers. Just because the church's speech cannot and will not be a religious variant of general propaganda, theological homiletics must needs imply an anti-homiletics.[103] In his critique of the publications of a former SS war correspondent, the Berlin German-scholar Peter Wapnewski writes: "Who can measure the effects of words, their responsibility in the events of history? 'Victory is really close at hand!'—how many bridge abutments may these words still have blown up, how many bazookas brought to the ready, how many white flags torn down—and how many men and women may have paid for these words with their lives, the killed, the hanged?"[104] Faced with such questions, which we can theologically convert and extend without undue strain, the Word-of-God hermeneutics is at the end of its rope. So we are asking: How many sermons on Romans 13 did it take to make Germany receptive for a crude metaphysics of the state? What effects did the formula of the two realms produce, what did it prevent? What sort of political consciousness does a catechism produce which, in the face of all the insights of socio-psychological research, patriarchally sticks the "superiors" and "rulers," etc., into the commandment on obedience to parents?[105] Does not the ideology of authorities, which Otto Heinrich von der Gablentz

---

[103] There is an abundance of material in the sources connected with the Hitler regime. In particular, cf. P. E. Schramm, ed., H. Picker, *Hitlers Tischgespräche im Führerhauptquartier 1941-1942* (Stuttgart, 1963); W. A. Boelke, ed., *Kriegspropaganda 1939-1941. Geheime Ministerkonferenzen im Reichspropagandaministerium* (Stuttgart, 1966); H. Boberach, ed., *Meldungen aus dem Reich. Auswahl aus den geheimen Lageberichten des Sicherheitsdienstes der SS 1939-1944* (Neuwied-Berlin, 1965). From a theological point of view, it is interesting to note in the *Sicherheitsdienst* reports the records of the effects of many a sermon.

[104] P. Wapnewski, "J. Fernau und die deutsche Seele," *Die Zeit*, 5 (1967), 18.

[105] Of outstanding quality here is the work of the Catholic pastoral theologian Th. Filthaut, who critically re-examines the Catholic catechism. Cf. Th. Filthaut, *Politische Erziehung aus dem Glauben* (Mainz, 1965), esp. 9 ff.: "Der Religionsunterricht—eine Gefahr für die Erziehung zur Demokratie?"

fittingly characterizes as the "mind-set of the unpolitical," [106] go hand in hand with the theological thinking about language that ignores the whole social dimension of language by ignoring linguistics? [107]

What the Americans W. L. Anderson and N. C. Stageberg are saying of their students also is to a large extent true of German theologians: "College freshmen are, for the most part, linguistically unsophisticated. Their attitudes toward language are often naïve; indeed, they have many misconceptions about language—misconceptions which they share with the general populace." [108] Two decades after Hitler, Goebbels, and their consorts, we can no longer excuse as gross negligence a service of the Word which is practiced naïvely and in an unsophisticated manner. If anyone is obligated to know the power and impotence of human words, then it is the guardian of the church's language. A light-footed appeal to God's own Word spoils everything; a sober analysis of language helps a lot. American research (Osgood, White) has uncovered the demagogic structure of Nazi propaganda through a quantitative statistical analysis of words.[109] Max Bense treats a language text as an expert in thermodynamics treats a gas—as a constant state in the medium of language.[110] Peter R. Hofstätter has worked out similarity relations and polarity profiles between concepts in various languages.[111] Such examples, which probably sound somewhat harsh for theological ears, may serve to demonstrate how far ahead of us fact-oriented research really is. The dogmatic appeal to the Word of God is premature so long as we do not know what the church is doing with the words and what the words are doing to the church. The appeal becomes a delict when it is used in ecclesiastical practice and by practical theology to create a dogmatic alibi in the face of a dismal reality of preaching.

Practical theology as the church's action-science is becoming cybernetical —understood not in the sense of Schleiermacher but of Norbert Wiener. In the feedback loop between practice and theological reflection practical theology takes the part of the game strategist; it is responsible for models of the structure and function of the church's behavior. We cannot expect from it assertoric sentences. It will have to avoid demanding formulations with definite value connotations, such as proclamation, gospel, address, assurance, etc., until these have been redefined. Meanwhile, its heuristic abstinence to-

[106] O. H. von der Gablentz, *Der Kampf um die rechte Ordnung. Beiträge zur politischen Wissenschaft* (Köln-Opladen, 1964), p. 123.

[107] So charges J. Barr, *Bibelexegese und moderne Semantik,* p. 279.

[108] Anderson and Stageberg, *Introductory Readings on Language,* p. vi.

[109] Research results in G. Maletzke, *Psychologie der Massenkommunikation,* p. 74; Cf. G. Herdan, *Language as Choice and Chance* (Groningen, 1956), pp. 45 ff.

[110] M. Bense, *Programmierung des Schönen. Allgemeine Texttheorie und Textästhetik* (Baden-Baden, 1960).

[111] P. R. Hofstätter, *Gruppendynamik. Kritik der Massenpsychologie* (Hamburg, 1965), 65 ff.

ward the Word of God benefits dogmatics. While practical theology does not teach certainty, it does lead the way toward reality. It does not strive for pure doctrine, but looks toward life which can never be "purely" experienced. We are not leaving behind Karl Barth's axiomatic Word because we despise it, but because we wish to regain it. But we can gain it only if we really need it. The road to the words would end in a hullabaloo, were we not able constantly to look back- and forward (dogmatically) for direction by the Word of God.

"The demand for pure doctrine does not imply that we refrain from, but that we fulfill, human words, sentences, chains-of-thought, and systematic relationships, so that they may be, not merely by force of negation but in their very reality, pure and therefore transparent. Precisely of such words it is demanded that they should serve the Word of God." [112] It follows from this demand that the reality of human words, sentences, and chains-of-thought, in their order or in their chaos, cannot be a matter of indifference to anyone who considers them in their transparency. Those who for good reason await the coming of the Word of God cannot very well trample all over the lexicon of men in which the Word of God is not contained, since God's Word neither speaks nor talks without our words. A theology which tolerates without resistance that those who are subhuman use the lexicon has lost its right of appealing to the Word. The always present contradiction between dogmatic pretension and empirical practice simply cannot be bridged or overcome theologically. It is imposed, not as an alibi, but as a challenge. As it fails methodologically, it may become clear to us that all theology takes place exclusively for the sake of men. To them the Word and the words are addressed.

[112] Barth, *Kirchliche Dogmatik*, I/2, 871.

III

THE LIVING GOD: A CHAPTER OF BIBLICAL THEOLOGY*

HANS-JOACHIM KRAUS

If a theologian intends to find a theologoumenon of the strongest assertive power to distinguish between the Christian doctrine of God and the "God of the philosophers," it is not infrequent that he employs the biblical designation "living God." Thus, for example, Martin Kähler, in opposition to the *deus absolutus* of a theology shaped by philosophy, spoke incessantly of the "living God" revealing himself and acting in history.[1] Speech of the "living God" also plays a definite role in Karl Barth's *Kirchliche Dogmatik*, especially in the doctrine of God which stresses that "God's being is *life*. Only the Living One is God. Only the voice of the Living One is God's voice. Only the work of the Living One is God's work. . . ."[2] Barth consistently refers to the "emphatic Old and New Testament designation of God as the 'living God.' . . ."[3] Without question we are dealing here with a significant theologoumenon.

I: *Contemporary Relevance and Problematic of the Theme*

The theme we have specified here with the biblical designation "living God" is particularly relevant today in several respects. The proclamation

---

* Translated by M. Douglas Meeks, Tübingen University, from *Evangelische Theologie,* 27:4 (April, 1967), pp. 169-200.

[1] Cf. the summary of J. Schniewind, "Der lebendige Gott in Martin Kählers theologischer Arbeit und biblischer Verkündigung," *Martin Kähler, Der Lebendige und seine Bezeugung in der Gemeinde,* ed. by Anna Kähler (Berlin, 1935). Schniewind himself appropriated this theologoumenon from his teacher. Cf. H.-J. Kraus, *Julius Schniewind—Charisma der Theologie* (Neukirchen-Vluyn, 1965), chap. VI: "Der lebendige Gott."

[2] K. Barth, *Kirchliche Dogmatik,* II/1 (4th ed., Zollikon-Zürich, 1958), 294-95.

[3] *Ibid.,* p. 295.

"God is dead" causes us to make fresh inquiries about the origin, the peculiarity, and the intended meaning of this theologoumenon rooted and developed in the Old Testament. There is also cause to confront the currently much discussed concept of "theism" at a crucial point with the biblical message.[4] In the current theological discussion about the God question, debated under various presuppositions and encumbrances, it is especially the Old Testament scholar who can only notice with astonishment how matter of factly and stubbornly the Old Testament is avoided in the discussion. The tendencies of a dualistically disposed "biblical theology," which are becoming more and more clearly distinguishable in New Testament scholarship, more or less exclude the Old Testament message from the current theological discussion. The consequence of such an attitude is the hasty readiness to pose the God question in agreement with or adjustment to other intellectual dimensions, insights, realities, and necessities and then to answer it correspondingly. If in this study, on the contrary, we first ask about the "living God" in the Old Testament, this nevertheless does not involve biblicistic tendencies which ignore present reality. Rather, it is an attempt to obtain pertinent and reliable information about "the issue of God" ("*die Sache mit Gott*"). One can only be astounded to realize that in the report by Heinz Zahrnt about twentieth-century Protestant theology (*Die Sache mit Gott*), everywhere extolled and praised for its reliability, Old Testament scholarship (which, if we only think of the work of Gerhard von Rad, has certainly not been experimenting in a hideaway) is totally missing—not even mentioned in one sentence. Furthermore, even the Old Testament itself is remembered now and then only in the immediate context at hand, and then quite on the periphery and far removed from every current issue or obligation.

But how can we speak of God and at the same time ignore the Old Testament? Reflection on the *biblical*-theological subject matter must be the point of departure for all working, thinking, and questioning. And this material substance of theology, in all "intellectual honesty" (which is today often affirmed to the point of boredom and with specific objectives in mind) should be the motor and fundamental principle of all theological research. If theologians no longer view themselves as engaged at this point, or only tenuously so, a philosopher can say to them: "All opportunities of the churches lie in the Bible if they are able to give them once again original expression today in awareness of the turning point of history" (Karl Jaspers).

We begin with the observation that the investigation of the Old Testament speech about the "living God" obviously contains a number of important problems in itself. Thus Ludwig Köhler, for example, explains in

[4] For these problems, cf. H. Gollwitzer, *Die Existenz Gottes im Bekenntnis des Glaubens* (4th ed., Munich, 1964), and H. G. Geyer, "Gottes Sein als Thema der Theologie," *Verkündigung und Forschung*, 11 (1966), 3 ff.

his *Theologie des Alten Testaments*: "The expression that God is a living God is found in the Old Testament only sparsely, late, and as a defense against the view that God has no life and power." [5] Köhler further maintains that while "our concept is commonly used, it has no clear and definite theological effect." [6] Does this explanation hit the nail on the head? Walther Eichrodt holds a different view: "Yahweh is called the *'ēl ḥay* (the "living God") rather early and emphatically and as such is again and again praised in his absolute superiority." [7] Edmond Jacob even places a whole chapter of his *Théologie de l'Ancien Testament* under the theme "Le dieu vivant" ("The Living God").[8] And finally Th. C. Vriezen emphasizes: "The theological witness of the Old Testament is decisively defined by the knowledge of the *living* God." [9]

How does this conspicuous disagreement come about? Certainly above all it results from the lack of a clear enough distinction between the narrow designation of Yahweh as *'ēl ḥay* and the broader theologoumenon. But it also results from promoting the variety of meanings issuing from the designation *'ēl ḥay* as fundamental theologoumena and with these attempting emphatically to comprehend and describe the totality of the Old Testament faith in God.

In any case, we must first of all try to establish exactly what meaning the designation of God in the Old Testament has in each particular formulation and each special context. Only then can we ask whether and to what extent the epithet "living God" is qualified to make basic theological statements about the God of the Old Testament and then also the God of the New Testament.

We must, however, immediately take note of and consider the fact that the phenomenology of religion forcefully allays and puts into question the emphasis of theological talk about the "living God." Nathan Söderblom entitled his Gifford Lectures, which he characterized as his "history of re-

[5] L. Köhler, *Theologie des Alten Testaments* (3rd ed., Tübingen, 1953), p. 86.
[6] *Ibid.*
[7] W. Eichrodt, *Theologie des Alten Testaments,* I (5th ed., Stuttgart and Göttingen, 1957), 136.
[8] E. Jacob, *Théologie de l'Ancien Testament* (Paris, 1955), pp. 28 ff.
[9] Th. C. Vriezen, *Theologie des Alten Testaments in Grundzügen* (Neukirchen, 1956), p. 141. J. Wellhausen also calls the God of Israel a "living God." He explains: "Only in opposition to the Canaanite nature gods he became truly the God of justice and of righteousness and thence, with the destruction of Israel by the Assyrians, the God of the world. Thus he was in fact a living God and his religion a progressing religion." *Israelitische und jüdische Geschichte* (9th ed., Berlin, 1959), p. 33. According to Wellhausen, Yahweh is therefore "living" *in his becoming, in the progress of the Israelite religion.* This is maintained under the presupposition: "Religion did not give the people participation in the life of the deity, but it gave the deity participation in the life of the people" (p. 33). We must question whether this view corresponds with the facts; whether the statements about the *'ēl ḥay* in the Old Testament can be understood in this way.

ligions legacy," *The Living God in the Witness of the History of Religions*.[10]
It is not only the God of the Old and New Testaments who is "living";
in all religious spheres, powers and gods prove themselves as "living" and
dynamically effective. They are understood as origin and source of all life.
Söderblom developed his lectures decisively on the basis of this conclusion.

In the present study it will, of course, not be possible to keep in view
the range and abundance of the data which can be brought into consideration by the phenomenology of religion. But it is therefore all the more
important to ascertain the special history of religions background of the
Old Testament designation *ēl ḥay*. Enduringly fundamental for posing the
history of religions question of the *'ēl ḥay* in the Old Testament is Wolf Graf
Baudissin's investigation *Adonis und Esmun,* which appeared in 1911 and to
which exegetes to this day refer. Baudissin saw the designation of God in
the Old Testament in relation to the multifarious background of the
Canaanite-Syrian religion with its dying and rising deities. Proof for the
"Canaanite origin" of the Old Testament speech of the "living God" could
not, of course, be produced.[11] But today we have at our disposal history of
religions texts which necessitate a scrutiny of Graf Baudissin's statements or
which teach us to see and explain the Old Testament designation of the
God of Israel within new contexts. These are especially texts from Egypt
and Ugarit, which we must carefully consider.

II: *The Oath Formula ḥay YHWH*

The best way to begin our investigation into the meaning of the designation *'ēl ḥay* ("living God") in the Old Testament would appear to be with
a discussion of the frequently appearing oath formula *ḥay YHWH* ("as
Yahweh lives"). This formula is used forty-two times in the Old Testament
texts as a ceremonial invocation.[12] It has also been identified in the Lachish
Ostraca (3:9; 12:3).[13] In addition, the invocations *ḥay 'ēl* ("as El lives")
(Job 27:2), and *ḥay 'ĕlōhîm* ("as Elohim lives") (II Sam. 2:27), are also
found in the Old Testament. *ḥay 'ānî* ("as I live") is used twenty-two times

[10] N. Söderblom, *Der lebendige Gott im Zeugnis der Religionsgeschichte* (Munich, 1942,
newly published in 1966). [Translator's note: The English title of these 1931 Gifford Lectures is *The Living God: Basal Forms of Personal Religion* (London, 1933).]

[11] W. Graf Baudissin, *Adonis und Esmun* (Leipzig, 1911), pp. 507-8. Already at this
point consideration of these hymnic amplifications amounts to a contradiction of Baudissin's
thesis (*ibid.*, p. 453, n. 1): The designation *ḥay* is to be understood only in the sense of
"living" (in antithesis to "dead") and expresses nothing about the active proof of the
life of Yahweh. L. Delekat's quite reserved lexicographical observations, *Vetus Testamentum*, XIV (1964), 27-28, which are essentially dependent on Baudissin, are also
inadequate.

[12] Cf. L. Köhler and W. Baumgartner, *Lexicon in Veteris Testamenti libros* (Leiden,
1953), pp. 291-92.

[13] H. Torczyner, *The Lachish Letters* (*Lachish I*), (Oxford, 1938).

as the words of Yahweh himself; Deut. 32:40 uses the words: *ḥay 'ānōkî lĕ'ōlām* ("as I live forever"). Attention should also be called to the phrase *ḥay naphšĕkā* ("as you live"), which occurs ten times in direct address. Finally, there is an oath in Gen. 42:15-16 which is sworn on the life of Pharaoh. This then is an overview of the uses of this concept.

It cannot be the task of this study to deal with the problem of the oath as it extends into the legal sphere. There have already been important investigations of this theme to which we can only refer.[14] To the extent, however, that an oath is a problem simultaneously in the phenomenology of religion and in theology, we must take up the main aspects of this relationship in our explanation of the invocation *ḥay YHWH*. But initially we want to limit the discussion to the scope of the Old Testament. In swearing an oath the *šēm YHWH* ("name of Yahweh") is called upon[15] and again in executing an oath. But an oath can also refer to the king.[16] And then, too, Yahweh swears by himself (cf. Ezek. 17:19; 33:11). We know that the gesture made in taking an oath involves the raising of the right hand "toward heaven." [17] How closely the gesture and the invocation are related can be seen in the oath to God in Deut. 32:40.

The Canaanites swear by Baal (Jer. 12:16). This brings up the question whether an invocation comparable to the *ḥay YHWH* oath was also used in the Canaanite realm. If this is the case, a further question is whether Israel possibly took the form of the invocation over from the original inhabitants of the country. We know of a cultic exclamation *ḥay 'al'iyan ba'al* ("as Aliyan Baal lives") attested to in the Ugaritic texts.[18] Was this exclamation also used as an invocation to taking an oath? It is possible. In any case, the formula "as Amon lives" was often used in Egypt,[19] and occasionally it was used in the combination, "as Amon lives and the king

[14] R. Hirzel, *Der Eid* (Leipzig, 1902): J. Pedersen, *Der Eid bei den Semiten* (Strassburg, 1914); F. Horst, "Der Eid im Alten Testament," *Evangelische Theologie*, 17(1957), 366 ff., republished in *Gottes Recht, Theologische Bücherei*, 12 (Munich, 1961), 292 ff.; F. Horst, "Eid," in *Die Religion in Geschichte und Gegenwart* (3rd ed., Tübingen, 1957), cols. 349-50.

[15] Lev. 19:12; Deut. 6:13; 10:20; I Sam. 20:42 *passim*.

[16] I Sam. 17:55; 25:26; II Sam. 11:11; 14:19.

[17] Gen. 14:22; Exod. 6:8; Pss. 68:31; 106:26; 144:8, 11; Ezek. 20:5 *passim*. [Translator's note: In Ezek. 20:5, the German translation reads: ". . . erhob ich meine Hand zu dem Samen des Hauses Jakob."]

[18] Cf. W. H. Schmidt, "Baals Tod und Auferstehung," *Zeitschrift für Religions- und Geistesgeschichte*, XV(1963), 1 ff. and the literature mentioned there. H. Ringgren, *Israelitisch-jüdische Religion* (Stuttgart, 1963), also asks concerning the invocation *ḥay YHWH*: "Is there any connection between this formula and the externally identical expression *ḥay 'al'iyan ba'al* . . .?" (p. 78). For swearing by alien deities, cf. also Amos 8:14-15.

[19] For this: J. A. Wilson, "The Oath in Ancient Egypt," *Journal of Near Eastern Studies*, 7(1948), 129 ff., and H. Bonnet, *Reallexikon der ägyptischen Religionsgeschichte* (Berlin, 1952), p. 164. As example from the texts one could mention: J. H. Breasted, *Ancient Records of Egyptian Historical Documents*, II (Chicago, 1927), § 58, p. 318.

lives." [20] The corresponding Old Testament invocation which refers to
Yahweh and the king (I Sam. 25:26) is perhaps of Egyptian origin. So
also the oath formula which refers to the king alone (I Sam. 17:55) [21] and
which in Gen. 42:15-16 has its Egyptian model. But in Mesopotamia, too,
a person who swears an oath calls upon the life of a deity or a king.[22] The
history of religions context in which the Old Testament invocation is to be
seen and understood is therefore unmistakable.

What significance does the invocation *hay YHWH* have in the Old Testament? This question must be answered with the background of the history
of religions continually in view. In the *Lexicon in Veteris Testamenti libros*,
Ludwig Köhler renders the meaning of this invocation (which has to be
translated "as Yahweh lives") with the interpretative statements: "God
is not to live, if . . ." or "the life of Yahweh is at stake." [23] The interpretation of the formula which deals with swearing "by the name of Yahweh"
should correspond to this meaning. The preposition *b* refers, according to
Köhler, to the valuables which are pledged if the oath refers to God.[24]
Josh. 2:14 might be summoned in support of this understanding. Here the
oath asserts: "Our life for yours!" (This means that the lives of those swearing the oath are offered as a pledge of forfeiture.) The invocation *hay
YHWH* would then set up the highest and strongest pledge of forfeiture,
the life of God, as the security for the truth of the oath.

Whether and to what extent such a conception can be proved to have
existed in the religious environment of Israel can scarcely be established or
decided. In any case, the interpretation is wrong for the Old Testament.
Friedrich Horst has shown this clearly in his study, "Der Eid im Alten Testament." [25] Even if men stake their lives on the truth of their oath in
Josh. 2:14, the following is still axiomatic with respect to the special invocation formula: "A person, however, never swears on his own life. This is
noteworthy and may prohibit attributing characteristics of a curse against the
self or pledge of forfeiture to this invocation formula which is always
placed independently before the real formulation of the oath." [26] But how
then is the formula *hay YHWH* to be understood? Horst offers a threefold explanation: "In the first place, one invokes the sphere of life, i.e., the
vital power of the deity, or of the man who exists in direct relationship to

[20] Cf. H. Bonnet, *Reallexikon*, p. 164. Bonnet explains that a sharpening of the oath was
apparently intended with this formula.

[21] Cf. also I Sam. 25:26; II Sam. 11:11; 14:19.

[22] B. Meissner, *Babylonien und Assyrien*, I (Heidelberg, 1920), 150, 176, and II (2nd
ed., 1925), 139. With reference to Thureau-Dangin, F. Horst points out that the particle of
swearing *niš* in the formula *niš ilim* or *niš šarrim* probably is to be derived from
nēšu="life" and not from *našû* (*qātam*)="to raise (the hand)"; (*Gottes Recht*, p. 307).

[23] *Lexicon in Veteris Testamenti libros*, pp. 292 and 943.

[24] *Ibid.*, p. 943.

[25] *Gottes Recht*, p. 307.

[26] *Ibid.*

God. Exactly this and no other power or potency is of concern here. Secondly, formulation takes place in such a way that the oath or oathlike guarantee with its own sphere is added and set next to that sphere of vital power as if it were brought into close contact with it. Finally, the guarantee must be spoken in contact with the sphere of vital power, and it does not only seek to compare its trustworthiness with the validity of the other sphere ("as X lives, such and such will take place . . .") insofar as it lives in and with and out of it." [27] These statements show an excellent grasp of the situation from a viewpoint of the phenomenology of religion. They are valid in principle for Israel as well as its religious environment. But a still more precise and more definite explanation must be sought which goes beyond the phenomena "life" and "power." It must try to formulate and to comprehend the unique character of the Old Testament invocation. The following points should serve this task.

1. It is clear that a person who calls upon the life of a deity withdraws from the context of magic. In the primitive understanding of life, an immanent nemesis rules in the realm of oath and curse.[28] "Inherent in the accomplished oath is a virulence which is inflamed when the oath is violated and which is extinguished as soon as the oath is fulfilled and, therefore, invalidated." [29] An oath's word of power evokes immediate effects in the realm of magic. When one calls upon the life of a deity in swearing, he yields and consecrates himself to this power.

2. The "living God" invoked in the formula becomes the *witness* to the oath. He is immediately present as the one solicited in the *šēm* ("name").[30] It must be asked here, however, under which presuppositions and how the invocation of the *šēm* in connection with the oath is to be understood. Is it a conjuring up of the deity which still implies magic elements? Or is the invocation of the *šēm* performed under the presupposition and on the basis of a gracious self-presentation and offer, as the Old Testament attests of the *šēm YHWH*? [31] Naturally it cannot and should not be denied that also in Israel the invocation of the *šēm* could have slipped away from the event which constituted and determined it and thus could have degenerated into misuse, magic sorcery, and depletion of its former content.[32] It is significant,

[27] *Ibid.*, p. 308.

[28] For the ancient oriental view of the "sphere of action which creates fate," in which an immanent nemesis holds sway, cf. G. von Rad, *Theologie des Alten Testaments*, I (4th ed., Munich, 1962), 278 ff., 397 ff., 424-25, and the literature mentioned there.

[29] F. Horst, *Gottes Recht*, p. 302. Cf. also S. Mowinckel, *Religion und Cultus* (Göttingen, 1953), pp. 65-66, and J. Pedersen, *Der Eid bei den Semiten*, pp. 150-51, or by the same author, *Israel*, III-IV (London, 1943), 450.

[30] For this: G. van der Leeuw, *Phänomenologie der Religion* (Tübingen, 1933), p. 135; also G. von Rad, *Theologie des Alten Testaments*, I, 195-96.

[31] For the revelation of the Yahweh-name in Israel, cf. G. von Rad, *Theologie des Alten Testaments*, I, 193 ff.

[32] The command of Exod. 20:7 is directed against this misuse (cf. G. von Rad, *Theologie des Alten Testaments*, I, 197); Hos. 4:15; Jer. 5:2.

however, that with the invocation *ḥay YHWH* Israel believed in the living presence and thus in Yahweh's being a witness. The passages in the Old Testament in which the God of Israel is designated as *'ēd* ("witness") must be applied to and considered for an explanation of the formula *ḥay YHWH*.[33] There are naturally difficulties involved in such an explanation with respect to texts in which the life of the king or—as can now be added —the life of the priest [34] or of the prophet [35] is called upon in the oath formula.

In Egypt the ruler was considered to be godlike. Attributing divine powers of omnipresence to him is self-evident to the person who swears an oath in his name. The formula of the "king's oath" (cf. I Sam. 25:26) in Israel may have been taken over from the Egyptians, as we have suggested. If this is indeed the case, it becomes necessary to ask what meaning this invocation can have had in the Old Testament world. One cannot exclude the possibility that the kings of Israel were considered and worshiped by the people as being godlike [36] or even themselves divine.[37] Then the oath sworn on the life of the king would be an expression of a folk piety (influenced by Egypt) and a reflex of the "style of the court" (also bearing the imprint of Egypt or of the ancient orient), which promotes the apotheosis of the regent. But it was also possible to swear by the life of a priest or prophet in Israel. This fact deserves consideration. We must then ask, did the Old Testament understand king, priest, and prophet as witnesses and representatives of the power of Yahweh? On this basis, could one invoke their lives? If so, these men would have been, by virtue of their offices, the present witnesses of Yahweh as "witness."

3. The significance of the invocation *ḥay YHWH* can be illustrated by the context of I Sam. 20:3, 21, where the oath formula can be ascertained. In vs. 23 reference is made to the swearing of the oath: "And as for the matter of which you and I have spoken, behold, the Lord is between you and me for ever" (cf. also vs. 42).

Yahweh is witness "between" those who declare the oath and in this way demonstrate his life, his living presence. But he *remains*—and the accent must lie here—as the watchman and the judge, the Living One for all time to come, the Lord over the word of the oath. The persons, among

[33] The following passages are involved: I Sam. 12:6; 20:12; Jer. 29:23; 42:5; Mic. 1:2; Zeph. 3:8; Mal. 3:5; Job 16:19. As witness God sees and hears what happens in the swearing; he is the "one who knows" (Jer. 29:23).

[34] In I Sam. 1:26 the priest Eli is called upon by his life.

[35] Cf. II Kings 2:2, 4, 6 (with reference to Elijah); II Kings 4:30 (with reference to Elisha).

[36] II Sam. 14:17 says (with respect to David): "My lord the king is like an angel of God to discern good and evil." And II Sam. 14:20 reads—and this statement is highly significant here: "My lord has wisdom like the wisdom of the angel of God *to know all things that are on the earth.*"

[37] In Ps. 45:6, the king is addressed with *'ĕlōhîm.*

whom Yahweh was present as *'ēd* ("witness") and becomes present as guardian of the oath in the future, place themselves under his power. Characteristic of this certainty which points to the future is the formulation: "God (or the gods) do so to me (or the one named) and more also!" [38] This form of speech interpreting the invocation may be of Canaanite origin.[39] If this is the case, then it should be stated at this point that the notion that God (or the deity) is in dynamic vitality a witness to an oath and a guardian and judge of this oath in case of default was determinative also for the religious environment of Israel.[40]

4. The formula *ḥay YHWH* should be understood as a *"word of consecration."* [41] The invocation is a solemn and powerful word. In some Old Testament passages in which the *ḥay YHWH* is exclaimed, a hymnlike amplification is connected to the formula in a participial construction or in a relative clause.[42] These amplifications are not to be dismissed, however, as solemn flourishes. They indicate in different ways and in various expressions where and how Yahweh, as the Living One who has been called upon in the invocation, has demonstrated his "life" and his vitality. These passages, then, elucidate Israel's belief in the "living God" and open the way to an understanding of the unique character of the Old Testament discourse about the phrase *'ēl ḥay* ("living God").

5. Were, when, and how did the God called upon with *ḥay YHWH* attest and demonstrate his life? This question can be answered with the following five references:

a) In Jer. 16:14-15 and 23:7-8, an assertion, which in connection with the "word of consecration" sounds hymnic and which has to be designated as a salvation history confession of Israel, is adjoined to the invocation *ḥay YHWH* in a relative clause. This confession speaks of God as one, ". . . who brought up the people of Israel out of the land of Egypt." The deuteronomic passage [43] has the lengthened invocation: "As the Lord lives

[38] Cf. I Sam. 3:17; 14:44; 20:13; II Sam. 3:9, 35; I Kings 2:23; Ruth 1:17 (plur. I Kings 19:2, 20:10).

[39] F. Baumgärtel, *Elohim ausserhalb des Pentateuch,* Theol. Dissertation (Leipzig, 1914), p. 61.

[40] This applies in Egypt: "With his oath the swearing one simultaneously sets himself under the vengeance of the god or of the king called upon. Occasionally this is expressly attested by supplements such as 'whose power will kill.' " H. Bonnet, *Reallexikon,* p. 164.

[41] Cf. G. van der Leeuw, *Phänomenologie der Religion,* p. 387 (the oath as "Form of the Word of Consecration").

[42] This occurs in I Sam. 14:39; 25:34; II Sam. 4:9; I Kings 1:29; 2:24; II Kings 3:14; 5:16; Jer. 16:14-15; 23:7-8; 38:16; Job 27:2. We should note here, however, that in the Ugaritic texts the personal name *ḥjil* is spoken of (J. Aistleitner, *Wörterbuch der ugaritischen Sprache* [Berlin, 1963], No. 917), and that an Egyptian sarcophagus text transmits the self-predication of the god Shu: "I am life, lord of the years, living to infinity, the lord of eternity . . ." (S. Morenz, *Ägyptische Religion* [Stuttgart, 1960], p. 153).

[43] For the literary critical and history of traditions questions, cf. S. Herrmann, *Die prophetischen Heilserwartungen im Alten Testament, Beiträge zur Wissenschaft vom Alten*

who brought up the people of Israel out of the land of Egypt." This is introduced like a well-known and current formula for an oath. But then it is stressed that this oath will no longer be used in the future and that the new invocation would be: "As the Lord lives who brought up the people of Israel out of the north country and out of all the countries where he had driven them."

One can scarcely doubt that the deuteronomist is actually quoting in Jer. 16:14 and 23:7 an extended invocation which was often used in Israel.[44] But this formula should be substituted, according to the deuteronomist's words, by a reformulation in connection with Yahweh's future work of salvation in the "new exodus."[45] In any case, Jer. 16:14-15 and 23:7-8 can be interpreted as showing that for Israel the life of Yahweh has been demonstrated in his fundamental deeds in the history of salvation and that it will be proved anew in the future.

b) In I Kings 2:24 another deed of Yahweh is attested in a clause which amplifies the invocation. Solomon introduces his oath with the words: "As the Lord lives who has established me, and placed me on the throne of David my father, and who has made me a house, as he promised. . . ." Here reference is made to the promise given through Nathan (II Sam. 7) and to its first fulfillment in the enthronement of Solomon. The deuteronomist points to the theme "promise and fulfillment"[46] with concrete reference to II Sam. 7. This indicates that Yahweh proves himself as the Living One in powerful historical deeds which are the fulfillment of his word of promise given in former times.

c) In the Elisha stories, the prophet adds to the oath which calls upon the living God the clause "whom I serve" (II Kings 3:14; 5:16). The serving stance of the prophet before Yahweh, his speech and his miraculous works, are an indication of the living power and presence of the God of Israel. One might also ask here (and with respect to I Kings 2:24 as well) whether such assertions about the relation of the prophet (or the king) to Yahweh open up an understanding of the oath invocation which calls on the life of one who is appointed by God or who serves in the presence of God.

d) In II Sam. 4:9 and I Kings 1:29, there is an amplification composed

---

und Neuen Testament, 85 (Stuttgart, 1965), 169, 170, n. 12. A. Weiser, on the contrary (*Das Alte Testament Deutsch,* 20), advocates the view that Jer. 16:14-15 are words of Jeremiah. This explanation seems unacceptable (cf. also W. Rudolph, *Jeremia, Handbuch zum Alten Testament,* 12 [Tübingen, 1953], under the relevant passages).

[44] Cf. also the generalizing extention in I Sam. 14:39: ". . . who saves Israel."

[45] For the "new exodus," which is proclaimed in the message of Deutero-Isaiah, cf. W. Zimmerli, "Der 'neue Exodus' in der Verkündigung der beiden grossen Exilspropheten," *Gottes Offenbarung, Theologische Bücherei,* 19 (Munich, 1963), 192 ff.

[46] Cf. W. Zimmerli, "Verheissung und Erfüllung," *Evangelische Theologie,* 12 (1952/53), 34 ff., and G. von Rad, *Theologie des Alten Testaments,* I, 346 ff.

in an *ad hoc* manner which is formulated in the style of an individual song of thanksgiving:[47] "As the Lord lives, who has redeemed my life out of every adversity." In both cases it is David who testifies with his confession of gratitude that Yahweh has shown his living and saving power to his servant. What has happened and what has been experienced explains the invocation *ḥay YHWH* in the form of a confession of hymnic character. In this confession the certainty that and how Yahweh lives is simultaneously confirmed. A similar *ad hoc* formulation is found in I Sam. 25:34, where the living power of Yahweh (connected to the formula *ḥay YHWH*) is indicated by the words: "For as surely as the Lord the God of Israel lives, who has restrained me from hurting you." Yahweh has shown his vitality in that, in some hidden way, he has changed the heart of David and thereby restrained him from committing an atrocious act. That the God of Israel was at work here has become self-evident to David (see the context).[48]

e) Jer. 38:16 contains an explanation of Yahweh's life-giving power which reaches into the fundamental principle of his creative bestowing of life. The passage begins with the invocation formula *ḥay YHWH* and then continues with the amplification: "who has made our lives" [the RSV reads "our souls"—Trans.]. The living God has given life to men and has thereby attested to his own liveliness.[49]

These five indications of the intended meaning of these amplifications of the formula *ḥay YHWH* very clearly demonstrate how in Israel the "life" of Yahweh was believed in and acknowledged and what ideas were combined with the invocation.[50]

III: *Yahweh Lives*

In Ps. 18:46, *ḥay YHWH* is not to be understood as the invocation connected with an oath, but as a hymnic exclamation.[51] At the conclusion of

---

[47] H. Gunkel/J. Begrich, *Einleitung in die Psalmen* (Göttingen, 1933), p. 7.

[48] In an extreme paradox, Job explains in the amplification of the invocation *ḥay YHWH* that Yahweh has taken away his right (Job 27:2). Even the God who seizes and who hides himself is witnessed here as the living God (cf. Job 1:21; 2:10).

[49] Cf. for this point the exposition in Part V: "The Fountain of Life."

[50] Here we can already point out the incorrectness of the above quoted view of L. Köhler that the assertion that God is a living God occurs in the Old Testament only sparsely, late, and in defense against the notion that God has no life and no power (*Theologie des Alten Testaments*, p. 86). Accepting this view would mean neglecting a whole area of Old Testament assertions, namely, the invocation *ḥay YHWH* with its significant amplifications.

[51] Cf. H.-J. Kraus, *Psalmen, Biblischer Kommentar*, XV/1 (3rd ed., Neukirchen Kreis Moers, 1966), see under the relevant passage. An objection by B. Duhm should be considered. In his *Psalmen-Kommentar*, Duhm defends the view that *ḥay YHWH* may not be translated "Yahweh is living" (reason: "since it does not fit here"), that the sentence rather contains only a reverential greeting (cf. *yĕḥî hammelek* in I Kings 1:39). The significance of *ḥay*, however, is supported today by the Ugaritic parallels (see below).

the individual song of thanksgiving, which is also found in II Sam. 22:47-49 in a parallel account, the singer rejoices:

> The Lord (Yahweh) lives; and blessed be my rock,
> and exalted be the God of my salvation,
> the God who gave me vengeance
> and subdued peoples under me;
> who delivered me from my enemies;
> yea, thou didst exalt me above my adversaries;
> thou didst deliver me from men of violence. (Ps. 18:46-48.)

The song of thanksgiving of the singer saved from his enemies modulates into a hymn of praise in vs. 46. It begins with the exclamation "Yahweh lives!" In recent research these two words have inspired a search for parallel expressions in the Canaanite-Syrian background now known through the Ugaritic texts. Here one encountered the already mentioned cultic-mythical exclamation *ḥay 'al'iyan ba'al,* on the basis of which some scholars have felt that the words *ḥay YHWH* in Ps. 18:46 must be seen and understood in association with the cult of the dying and rising gods. Especially George Widengren views Ps. 18 as interwoven with ancient Canaanite motifs and interprets it accordingly.[52]

These history of religious observations and statements (as insufficiently differentiated as many of them may be) come to a focal point in the following question: Was Yahweh also worshiped in ancient Israel as a dying and rising deity? Does accordingly the exclamation *ḥay YHWH* refer to a resurrection of Yahweh? Does Israel, too, belong to the sphere of influence of a "pattern," a mythical-cultic scheme, which is supposed to have dominated the entire ancient Orient?

Apart from the special context containing the invocation of Yahweh in an oath, the exclamation *ḥay YHWH* can be ascertained in the Old Testament only in Ps. 18:46.[53] This fact seems to make it problematic from the outset to attribute to the cultic-mythical theory a significant interpretative value for Old Testament texts. Widengren is correct, however, when he asserts that one must not deal here just with God's "dying and rising," but also with his "sleeping and awakening." [54]

In Ugarit the dead Baal is also described as the sleeping one, and the rising Baal as the awakening one. From this point of view, the Old Testament

---

[52] G. Widengren, *Sakrales Königtum im Alten Testament und im Judentum* (Stuttgart, 1955), pp. 69 ff. For the Canaanite elements in Ps. 18, cf. W. F. Albright, *Archaeology and the Religion of Israel* (Baltimore, 1941), p. 129. Albright calls this psalm "canaanizing."

[53] For the formula *ḥay gō'ālî* in Job 19:25, see below.

[54] G. Widengren, *Sakrales Königtum,* pp. 67 ff. W. Graf Baudissin, *Adonis und Esmun,* pp. 403 ff., had already called attention to these associations. Cf. also F. F. Hvidberg, *Graad og Latter i det Gamle Testamente* (Copenhagen, 1938), pp. 109 ff.

material which can be considered and investigated with the history of religions methodology is considerably enriched. The most important passages are the following: A person in need asks Yahweh in his prayer, "Why sleepest thou?" (Ps. 44:23). The corresponding requests of the individual lamentations are: "Arise, O Lord!" (Pss. 7:6; 9:19; 10:12), "Awake, O my God" (Pss. 7:6; 35:23; 44:23; 59:4; Isa. 51:9). Ps. 78:65 reports that Yahweh "awoke as from sleep." All these passages must be considered if the exclamation ḥay YHWH in Ps. 18:46 is to be appropriately explained.

A very brief summary dealing with the *religious environment of Israel* is appropriate at this point. Three important cultic-mythical complexes must be indicated in which the dying and rising deities were worshiped.

1. An impressive example of Canaanite-Syrian cult and myth is presented in the Ras Shamra texts.[55] When the land is dried out and the vegetation is wilted by the summer drought, the god of death, Mot, is dominant. Baal, the god of rain and fruitfulness, has died; he sleeps. The god El leaves his throne and begins to sing the ritual lament to mourn the dead god:

> Baal is dead!
> What shall become of the sons of Dagon?
> What shall become of the host of Baal?
> I will descend into the earth.[56]

Baal's wife and sister, Anat, weeps as she seeks the dead god. She finds him in the depth of the underworld and drags his body to the heights of Zaphon. When the period of the winter rains begins and after a hard struggle with Mot, Baal rises from the dead. The certainty first expressed by El holds sway:

> Aliyan Baal lives!
> The prince exists, the Lord of the earth! [57]

This mythic event is present in the cult; it is celebrated, recited, and dramatically enacted.

2. Some elements of this Baal-Mot cycle remind us of the Egyptian Isis-Osiris myth, especially as it has become known through the narratives of Plutarch.[58] While, however, in Ugarit the resurrection of Baal, the "lord of the earth," brings new fertility to the fields and the power of life to men, in Egypt we find an almost

---

[55] For this: W. H. Schmidt, *Königtum Gottes in Ugarit und Israel,* Beiheft zur *Zeitschrift für die alttestamentliche Wissenschaft,* 80 (2nd ed., Berlin, 1966), 10 ff. W. H. Schmidt, "Baals Tod und Auferstehung," where additional lit. is given.

[56] W. H. Schmidt, "Baals Tod und Auferstehung," p. 3.

[57] *Ibid.,* p. 9.

[58] Cf. Th. Hopfner, *Plutarch über Isis und Osiris,* I, II, *Monographien des Archiv Orientální,* IX (1940/41); E. Otto/M. Hirmer, *Osiris und Amun* (Munich, 1966); W. Helck, "Osiris," in Pauly-Kroll-Ziegler, *Lexikon der Antike* (Stuttgart, 1962 ff.). Suppl. IX, cols. 469 ff.

mystical identification of the individual, especially the king, with Osiris. In a sarcophagus inscription the deceased says,

> I live, I die: I am Osiris. I have entered into
> you and have emerged from you.
> I have become fat in you, I have grown in you.
> I have fallen on my side. The gods live off me.
> I live and I grow as Nepre, who takes away those
> worthy of honor. Geb has hidden me.
> I live, I die, I am the barley. I do not pass away.[59]

E. Otto explains that "the cycle of the grain seed, which sinks into the soil, swells and sprouts there, and is 'resurrected' in a new plant, offered a consoling analogy for man. It became for him a symbol of 'immortality.' This, of course, guaranteed neither salvation from death nor a bodily resurrection, but the continuation of life." [60]

3. In Mesopotamia the equivalent of the cult of the dying and rising gods is represented by the Tammuz ritual. We can only note the most important literature.[61]

In the religious manifestations of Israel's environment, the power of myth played a dominant role. "Its content is the life of nature with its tensions and movements, conceiving and bearing, the masculine and feminine primal powers with their joy and suffering of love, being born, having to die, and rising up again in the plant world, producing and destroying, the variation and the battle among the elements, attracting and repulsing, the interrelation and the opposition of above and below, heaven and earth, the bubbling up and the drying up of the springs—the great rhythm which never ceases as long as the earth remains, of seedtime and harvest, cold and heat, summer and winter, day and night." [62]

One simply does not gain an understanding, however, of those passages in the Old Testament (primarily in the psalms) in which Yahweh is spoken of as "sleeping" and "rising" or as "living," from these mythological phenomena.[63] Single words and statements in the Old Testament are, of course, taken over from Israel's religious environment, but they are placed in a new context of expression and of meaning. It should be especially noted that in songs of lament, in which the suffering man at prayer finds himself at the most extreme distance from God, the *hiddenness of Yahweh* is viewed parabolically as "sleep." A "death" of Yahweh is never spoken of. "Sleep"

[59] Otto/Hirmer, *Osiris und Amun*, p. 28.
[60] *Ibid.*, p. 23.
[61] P. M. Witzel, *Tammuz-Liturgien und Verwandtes, Analecta Orientalia*, 10 (1935); A. Falkenstein/W. von Soden, *Sumerische und akkadische Hymnen und Gebete* (Zürich, 1953), pp. 185 ff.; H. Schmökel, *Heilige Hochzeit und Hoheslied* (Leipzig, 1956).
[62] W. Vischer, *Das Christuszeugnis des Alten Testaments*, II (Munich, 1942), p. 373.
[63] So also H. Ringgren, *Israelitische Religion*, pp. 78-79; W. H. Schmidt, "Baals Tod und Auferstehung," p. 4 n. 23; E. Jacob, *Théologie de l'Ancien Testament*, p. 29.

in these psalms is therefore an image for the attitude of the *deus absconditus*, of the God who is silent and does not intervene, who does not—not yet—demonstrate his life and power to those whose spirit is broken.

If we were to read into the special situation of the individual lamentations [64] a relevant mythical element, we would disregard the unambiguous intended meaning of these psalms. We would simply select the words and phrases which sound mythical in order to arrange them into a structure ("pattern") which is taken over from alien realms. But the problematic of this phenomenology of religions eclecticism is most clearly apparent in the fact that the *antitheses*, which we find in the Old Testament as clothed in the speech patterns of the religious environment, are no longer perceived.

In Ps. 18:46, the exclamation "Yahweh lives!" in the context of the song of thanksgiving definitely has the primary intention of praising the saving power of Yahweh who has demonstrated himself in his intervention as "living." [65] But the hymnic parts of a song of thanksgiving elevate both what is experienced and what is learned to the rank of undeniable universality. When such an expression of doxology, which strives to establish its point so absolutely, is formulated in a statement that sounds like the Baal myth, the polemic force cannot be ignored or overlooked. The life of Yahweh is manifested in his dynamic interventions into the history of his people and his servants.

These antithetical foci can be best demonstrated in Ps. 121:3-4 and Hab. 1:12 where they are sharply formulated by aimed negations. The Baalim are asleep;[66] they are subject to the rhythm of growth and decay. The prayer of the psalmist confesses and instructs:

> My help comes from the Lord,
> Who made heaven and earth.
> He will not let your foot be moved,
> he who keeps you will not slumber.
> Behold, he who keeps Israel
> will neither slumber nor sleep. (Ps. 121:2-4.)

The "keeper of Israel" does not sleep.[67] In his action on and in Israel, Yahweh has proved his wakefulness and his life in history. This God is believed in and recognized as the creator of heaven and earth. His utter watchfulness

---

[64] Cf. H. Gunkel/J. Begrich, *Einleitung in die Psalmen*, §6. In view of form historical researches we must bear in mind that every disregard of the class in which a statement is found and in whose context it must be explained and understood has distorting consequences.

[65] Cf. H.-J. Kraus, *Psalmen*, under the passage.

[66] Cf. I Kings 18:27.

[67] For Ps. 121, see: J. Morgenstern, "Psalm 121," *Journal of Biblical Literature*, 58 (1939), 311 ff.; P. H. Pollock, "Psalm 121," *ibid.*, 59 (1940), 411 ff.; O. Eissfeldt, "Psalm 121," *Festschrift für H. Lilje* (Hamburg, 1959).

and unlimited power are granted to each individual. The believer can and should be certain that God lives.

The words of Hab. 1:12 are hymnic:

> Art thou not from everlasting,
> O Lord my God, my 'Holy One' [68]
> Who shall not die? [69]

Here the Old Testament antithesis to the belief in the gods of the religious environment and the opposition to hopelessness in Israel is clearly expressed: *Yahweh does not die*. He has been living as the holy God from everlasting, separated in his holiness from all temporal, mortal beings. Karl Elliger makes some very good comments: "One must keep in mind that Israelite thought is not concerned with an eternity of pure being, but rather an eternity of activity. To be is to be vital, active, effective. It is not accidental that 'shall not die' corresponds to 'from eternity' in the parallel construction. Interest is expressed not just in the beginning and ending points of mere existence as such, but, parallel to the conception of God's not sleeping (Ps. 121:3), in the dynamic being-at-work in the entire period between these polarities and especially in the present." [70]

As the Living One *Yahweh "watches" over his word* (Jer. 1:12). In a calamitous vision, the coming judgment over Judah and Jerusalem is announced to the prophet Jeremiah (Jer. 1:13 ff.). What will come from this prophecy of judgment? Will it be realized in deeds, will it be "fulfilled"? Yahweh assures his prophet that he will "watch" over his word, once it has been proclaimed, and will accompany it to its fulfillment. Yahweh's living power is demonstrated in the fact that his word which announces can exist for a long time in the space of history, but will effectively assert itself at the proper time. Even under the trials of God's silence and of his apparent inactivity the prophet should not think that Yahweh were sleeping, were dead. He lives and is awake, is watching.

Job 19:25 should be mentioned here where *ḥay gō 'ălî* ("my redeemer lives") has a certain similarity with *ḥay YHWH* of Ps. 18:46, but this can only be understood when attention is given to the special situation in the dialogues of the book of Job. Job contends:

> I know that my redeemer lives,
> and at last he will stand upon the earth.

[68] For the revision of the text, cf. *Biblia Hebraica*, ed. R. Kittel.

[69] Present in the Hebraic transmission of the text is a *tiqûn sōphĕrîm*, a revision undertaken for dogmatic reasons. This revision sets aside the notion that God would be able "to die" even when the "not-dying" of God is mentioned. For the revision, cf. *Biblia Hebraica*.

[70] K. Elliger, *Die Propheten Nahum, Habakuk, Zephanja, Haggai, Sacharja, Maleachi*, in *Das Alte Testament Deutsch*, 25 (5th ed., Göttingen, 1964), see under the passage.

We cannot discuss here the difficult exegetical problems. It is enough to note that Job penetrates the terrifying experience that Yahweh is silent and is his enemy, and solemnly appeals to his savior: "God the surety." He is certain that this helper "lives" and that he will lead his cause to victory.[71]

IV: 'ĕlōhîm ḥayyîm

The invocation ḥay YHWH had its established place in the oaths of all periods in Israel. The Old Testament passages discussed in the third part of this essay, with their Canaanite words and phrases, are situated within the sphere of cultic tradition. But the designations of Yahweh as 'ĕlōhîm ḥayyîm or 'ēl ḥay, to which we now shift our attention, are found in scattered and various kinds of contexts within the Old Testament. An overview basically proffers the following picture:

> 'ĕlōhîm ḥayyîm: I Sam. 17:26; Deut. 5:26; Jer. 10:10; 23:36 (Aramaic: Dan. 6:21, 26); 'ĕlōhîm ḥay: II Kings 19:4, 16.
> 'ēl ḥay: Josh. 3:10; Hos. 1:10; Pss. 42:2; 84:2.

Our task is now to explain these passages. For the moment we are setting aside Pss. 42:2 and 84:2, however, since they deal with a designation of the God of Israel which must be seen and understood in particular contexts, as will be shown in Part V.

Let us begin with I Sam. 17:26:

> And David said to the men who stood by him,
> "What shall be done for the man who kills this
> Philistine, and takes away the reproach from Israel?
> For who is this uncircumcised Philistine, that he should
> defy the armies of the living God?"

We find this speech of David in the well-known David and Goliath story. The interpretation of this story is made especially difficult by repetitions and contradictions in the traditional text (which contains considerable variations from the Septuagint).[72] Probably two different traditions are blended here.[73] If it is correct that the "older form" is present in vss. 20-30,[74] then the passage cited would be a component of this older form.

[71] Cf. G. von Rad, *Theologie des Alten Testaments*, I, 428.

[72] Cf. P. A. H. de Boer, "I Sam. 17: Notes on the Text and the Ancient Versions," *Old Testament Studies*, 1(1942), 79-104; de Boer, "Research into the Text of I Samuel 17-31," *ibid.*, 6 (1949), 1-100; H. J. Stoebe, "Die Goliathperikope I Samuel 17:1-18:5 und die Textform der Septuaginta," *Vetus Testamentum*, 6 (1956), 397 ff.

[73] H. Gressmann, *Die älteste Geschichtsschreibung und Prophetie Israels, Die Schriften des Alten Testaments in Auswahl*, II/1 (2nd ed., Göttingen, 1921), 70.

[74] *Ibid.*, pp. 70-71.

Nothing here speaks in favor of a deuteronomistic insertion.[75] But, turning to the content: Goliath has mocked the armies of the "living God." How is the use of *'ĕlōhîm ḥayyîm* to be understood in this passage? H. W. Hertzberg contrasts the Philistine as the "worshiper of *dead* gods" (I Sam. 5) with Israel, the hosts of the *living* God.[76] H. Gressmann comments somewhat differently: "Israel's wars are Yahweh's wars (18:17, 25:28); Israel's enemies, Yahweh's enemies (30:26; Judg. 5:31); Israel's hosts, Yahweh's hosts (vs. 45). Whoever mocks Israel, mocks Yahweh, the "living God" (vss. 26, 36; II Kings 19:4, 16; Jer. 10:10)." [77] These expository sentences describe well the circumstances here. The reference to II Kings 19:4, 16 is especially important because it deals with a scene which is quite similar.[78] Referring to von Rad's study of holy war in ancient Israel,[79] we can assert the following: Yahweh shows himself as the living God in his powerful interventions in the holy war. Whoever then mocks the hosts of Israel defies the *'ĕlōhîm ḥayyîm*, who is present in this instrument of his deeds. As regards I Sam. 17:26, it cannot be established with certainty to what extent this use of the proof of the life of Yahweh as a contrast to the "dead gods" forms a decisive accent. But the fact must be considered that in the religious environment of Israel, as far as we know, a deity was never referred to in this way as "living." [80]

I Sam. 17:26 is probably the oldest passage in which *'ĕlōhîm ḥayyîm* is mentioned. About Hos. 1:10, it must be said that this first verse of the announcement of salvation (1:10–2:1) is much disputed:

> Yet the number of the people of Israel
> shall be like the sand of the sea,
> which can be neither measured
> nor numbered; and in the place where
> it was said to them,
> "You are not my people,"
> it shall be said to them,
> "Sons of the living God."

[75] W. Caspari seems to be in favor of a deuteronomistic formulation: *Die Samuelbücher, Kommentar zum Alten Testament,* VII (Leipzig, 1926), 204.

[76] H. W. Hertzberg, *Die Samuelbücher,* in *Das Alte Testament Deutsch,* 10 (3rd ed., Göttingen, 1965), see under the passage.

[77] *Ibid.,* p. 73.

[78] II Kings 19:4, 16 also speaks of a reviling of the "living God," and indeed by the Assyrian Sennacherib. Yahweh as the Living One is asked to open his eyes and ears in order to recognize and punish the atrocity (vs. 16).

[79] G. von Rad, *Der heilige Krieg im alten Israel* (Göttingen, 1951).

[80] W. Graf Baudissin, *Adonis und Esmun,* pp. 507-8, and Chr. Barth, *Die Errettung vom Tode in den individuellen Klage- und Dankliedern des Alten Testaments* (Zollikon-Zürich, 1947), p. 40. The formula *ḥay 'al'iyan ba'al* is related to the God who has come to life *again.* One will also not be allowed to introduce at this point the Ugaritic statement that El has "eternal life"; cf. Part V in this connection.

A. Weiser [81] and H. W. Wolff [82] see these verses as coming from Hosea, while S. Herrmann [83] has relegated them to "the theology of the period of the Exile." The importance of H. W. Wolff's question concerning Hos. 1:10—2:1 is not to be underestimated: "Is it not more difficult to suppose that the free alteration of the name 'my People' into 'Sons of the living God,' the entirely new application of the name of Jezreel as well as the conception of the children as 'brothers' and 'sisters' was carried out by a later editor who added material from Ezechiel's world of thought to Hosea's message? Is not all this much more difficult to understand than merely supposing this belongs to Hosea's own thought?" [84] There is much reason for ascribing Hos. 1:10—2:1 to Hosea himself. What significance then would naming the Israelites "sons of the living God" have? Here the placing of the two ideas over against each other must first be considered. "Not my people" means Israel in the process of going back on the covenant and the judgment. But Yahweh does not die with Israel. He is God and not a man (Hos. 11:9). He is Lord over the life and death of his people (Hos. 6:1-3; 13:14; Deut. 32:39; I Sam. 2:6). As the Living One, Yahweh demonstrates himself to his "sons," [85] by accepting once more those whom he had rejected and renewing his covenant with them (Hos. 2:20). Therefore we can follow H. W. Wolff's explanation here: "The new name 'sons of the living God' was originally formulated by Hosea." The contrary image would be "the children of harlotry" (Hos. 1:3 ff.; 2:4), "who are indebted to an alien god for their lives and who consequently fall heir to death in judgment." [86]

We encounter a characteristic piece of deuteronomic theology in Deut. 5:26:

> For who is there of all flesh, that has heard
> the voice of the living God speaking out of the midst
> of fire, as we have, and has still lived?

The deuteronomist poses this question in the paraenetic paraphrases of the Sinai tradition.[87] A direct encounter between flesh and God means death (Exod. 33:20). Israel, however, experienced God in two different ways on Sinai. *'ĕlōhîm ḥayyîm* was revealed to her as living in his *qōl*, in his voice

[81] A. Weiser, *Das Buch der Zwölf Kleinen Propheten, I*, in *Das Alte Testament Deutsch*, 24 (Göttingen, 1963), see under the passage.

[82] H. W. Wolff, *Dodekapropheton I. Hosea, Biblischer Kommentar*, XIV/1 (2nd ed., Neukirchen Kreis Moers, 1965), see under the passage.

[83] S. Herrmann, *Die prophetischen Heilserwartungen im Alten Testament* (Stuttgart, 1965), p. 117 n. 39.

[84] *Ibid.*, p. 28.

[85] Cf. Exod. 4:22; Hos. 11:1; Deut. 14:1; 32:19.

[86] S. Herrmann, *Die prophetischen Heilserwartungen*, p. 30. Cf. Hos. 5:7; 9:10 ff.; 11:7; 13:1.

[87] Cf. G. von Rad, *Das fünfte Buch Mose*, in *Das Alte Testament Deutsch*, 8 (Göttingen, 1964), see under the passage.

which came out of the fire. But this God did not kill; as the Unapproachable and the Living One he let those to whom he spoke live. The *'ĕlōhîm ḥayyîm* received this special character in the context of the Sinai tradition.[88] It can be shown then that the deuteronomic-deuteronomistic theology took up the epithet *'ĕlōhîm ḥayyîm* or *'ēl ḥay* and accented assertions about the God of Israel with his designation.

The speech of Joshua in Josh. 3:10-11 is deuteronomistic:[89]

> And Joshua said, "Hereby you shall know that the living
> God is among you, and that he will without fail
> drive out from before you the Canaanites, the Hittites,
> the Hivites, the Perizzites, the Girgashites, the
> Amorites, and the Jebusites. Behold, the ark of the
> covenant of the Lord of all the earth is to pass over
> before you into the Jordan.

The formula of recognition [90] introduces Joshua's speech. A demonstration is to take place in the history of Israel. The prophesying and disclosing word proclaims the wonderful intervention of the living God. In that the Jordan is crossed by the "ark of the covenant" and the promised land is entered,[91] Yahweh, the *'ēl ḥay*, proves himself to be *'ădōn kol-hā'ārez* ("Lord of all the earth," vs. 11).

Jer. 23:36 must also be viewed as deuteronomistic. The pseudo-prophets, which are dealt with in Jer. 23:9 ff,[92] have perverted "the words of the living God, the Lord of hosts, our God." In the message of the prophets sent and authorized by Yahweh, the *'ĕlōhîm ḥayyîm* is manifest. The sacrilege of the pseudo-prophets is exposed in its abysmal dreadfulness, in that the words of the living God are "perverted." The pseudo-prophets forcibly place these words at their own disposal. The living efficacy of Yahweh is no longer known in these circles. They have made Yahweh into an idol, into a "dead God" whose *dābār* (word) can be twisted and turned according to their whims. Thus we can see a clear emergence of that contrast which is sharply formulated in Jer. 10:10 and which became prevalent in later periods as a characteristic theologoumenon:

> But the Lord is the true God;
> He is the living God and the everlasting King.

[88] Also in Deut. 4:33 *ḥayyîm* has to be added behind *'ĕlōhîm* (cf. *Biblia Hebraica*).
[89] Cf. M. Noth, *Das Buch Josua, Handbuch zum Alten Testament*, 1/7 (2nd ed., Tübingen, 1953), see under the passage.
[90] For the "recognition formula," cf. W. Zimmerli, *Erkenntnis Gottes nach dem Buche Ezechiel, Abhandlungen zur Theologie des Alten und Neuen Testaments*, 27 (Zürich, 1954).
[91] For the cultic and cult-historical problems of the passage through the Jordan, cf. H.-J. Kraus, *Gottesdienst in Israel* (Munich, 1962), pp. 179 ff.
[92] Cf. H.-J. Kraus, *Prophetie in der Krisis, Biblische Studien*, 43 (Neukirchen-Vluyn, 1964), 20 ff.

The tenth chapter of Jermiah cannot be attributed to Jeremiah. One recognizes deuteronomistic elements in this passage which is primarily a hymnic piece. But it is no doubt dependent on Deutero-Isaiah in its essential thoughts and motives.[93] Yahweh, in his dynamic vitality, is placed over against the impotent, dead idols. The God of Israel is incomparable (vs. 6). His uniqueness is expressed with the designations *'ĕlōhîm ḥayyîm* and *melek 'ōlām* ("everlasting King").[94] The "dead idols," on the other hand, are the creations of man (vs. 14), who shows his stupidity and lack of knowledge in his religious zeal (vs. 14). The living might of Yahweh, however, is made known in that he, as the "King of the nations" (vs. 7) and the Creator of the world (vs. 12), lets his wrath go forth upon the earth and, with his intervention, exposes the religious vanity of men (vss. 14 ff.). While the idols cannot bestir themselves, Yahweh, as the Living One, is Lord of all life (W. Rudolph).

Finally, we must note the effect of this theology in the apocalyptic writings. In Dan. 6:20, Daniel is described as "servant of the living God."[95] Associated with the "living God" is the expectation that he can *rescue* his servant from the lions' den. One may expect deliverance by the "living God" even in extreme need. After the rescue has taken place and fear and worship are by order of the king to be attributed to the God of Daniel as his due, the hymnic argument runs:

> For he is the living God,
> enduring forever;
> his kingdom shall never be destroyed,
> and his dominion shall be to the end.
> He delivers and rescues,
> he works signs and wonders
> in heaven and on earth. (Dan. 6:26-27.)

Later in the stories of "Belshazzar of Babylon"[96] and the "Dragon of Babylon,"[97] a harsh contrast to the "living God" is presented by the dead idols of the pagans.[98]

In retrospect now it can be established that most of the (hymnic)

---

[93] Different from Weiser (*Das Buch des Propheten Jeremia*, in *Das Alte Testament Deutsch*, 20 [Göttingen, 1960]), who reflects on a tradition of worship which in the proclamation of Jeremiah became acute through politics of religion of Manasseh and Jehoiachin.

[94] The kingship of Yahweh is therefore an unchanging, enduring rule. This designation corresponds to the Yahweh-King hymns in which it is not an "enthronement of Yahweh" which is praised, but rather the "eternal kingship" of Yahweh (cf. Ps. 93:2).

[95] Cf. with this, II Kings 3:14; 5:16.

[96] "Bel and the Dragon," vss. 3 and 4.

[97] *Ibid.*, vss. 23 and 24.

[98] According to II Macc. 7:33, the God of Israel proves his aliveness by his punishing and educative rule over his people. He is the "Living Lord" in anger and in grace.

amplifications of the oath invocations (cf. Part II) are in basic agreement
in their intended meaning with what has been ascertained from the discussion
of 'ĕlōhîm ḥayyîm in Part IV. Accordingly, then, in the exclamatory oath
ḥay YHWH, what Israel proclaimed, believed, and knew about the living
God who proved himself dynamic in history, resounds with the invocation
and supplements it by changing accentuation. Thus it cannot be substantiated
that the assertion that Yahweh is a "living God" appears in the Old Testament late and sparsely. This phrase was formulated at an early date as an
antithesis to the dying and dead gods of Israel's environment. It was used
in proclamation, confession, and hymn, and it was repeated in differing
circumstances. This polemic can only become effective, however, on the
basis of faith's experience of the living power of Yahweh who determines
history, accompanies it, and proves himself in it. There is also no doubt that
the God of Israel was experienced *personally* as the "Living One." [99] His
majestic, incomparable "I" who promises and fulfills, acts and leads, inter-
venes and watches, is no anonymous numinous reality, but an acting person:
a person whom Israel (and within Israel, the individual person) was expected
and in duty bound to listen to, obey, call upon, honor and praise. But this
"I" *cannot be compared* with any other (Hos. 11:9; Jer. 10:6). His person-
hood is essentially the turning of the living divine being toward mankind.
It is the deed of deliverance and judgment, of waking and guiding, of faithfulness and patience.[100]

So it is not just a matter of determining *that* the God of Israel is a person.
Rather, the decisive issue is exactly as *what* person he makes himself known
in his revelation and thus in his deeds.[101] In trying to answer this question,
he who hears and considers it quickly becomes aware that, to the extent that
he encounters *God*, he is not able to find any definitions. The theologoumenon
"living God" points to the speaking and acting of Yahweh in the history

[99] "Saying of God that he was a living God, was the elementary and primordial re-
action of man before the experience of the power which, in imposing itself on the totality
of his person, could only be envisioned as a person, that is to say, as a living being."
E. Jacob, *Théologie de l'Ancien Testament*, p. 29.

[100] E. Käsemann emphasizes: "Revelation ceases to be God's revelation once it has been
brought within a causal nexus. It is what it is only when it is seen as an irreducible encounter." *Exegetische Versuche und Besinnungen*, I (4th ed., Göttingen, 1965), 200. Insofar
as "one" brings God's revelation into a casual nexus, Käsemann's critical assertions are
correct. But in the Old Testament Israel experiences its God's faithfulness and constancy,
his aliveness and historical power in an encounter which is grounded in Yahweh's faithfulness to his covenant—and is therefore not "irreducible." The *causa fidelitatis*, standing
under its own presuppositions and grounded in God himself, creates and opens up ker-
ygmatically transmitted and confidently believed *contexts* in which God has made himself
present. What takes place in the Old Testament cannot and may not be dissolved—as
widely happens—by an eschatological actualism and existential punctualism in which
the fear that man might be able to put God's revelation at his disposal is stronger than
the joy in the faithfulness of the living God and in his historical power.

[101] Cf. K. Barth, *Kirchliche Dogmatik*, II/1, 333.

of his people and of the peoples of the world. It refers to his speaking and acting which occur in sovereign *freedom* and in *faithfulness to his covenant* which survives the generations, is continually present, and demonstrates itself ever anew. That "God" is "dead" is a "mythologoumenon" of pagan religiosity in the magic circle of growth and decay. But it is also a judgment of faith about the gods of the nations. That the God of Israel lives is the kerygma, confession of belief, and praise of the people of God.

V: *The Fountain of Life*

In our investigation of the traceable amplifications of the invocation *ḥay YHWH* in the Old Testament, we encountered (among others) the formulation in Jer. 38:16, "As the Lord lives, who made our lives" [or "our souls"]. While mention of the "living God" in the majority of cases relates to Yahweh's dynamic rule in history and his demonstration of his life through and in Israel, in Jer. 38:16 another notion emerges: the living God is creator and dispenser of life. With this we meet a theme complex which the Old Testament indicates in terms of the image and simile that Yahweh is the "fountain of life." [102] Concerning the context of this theme in the phenomenology of religion, we can assert with Christoph Barth: "Life of every kind has its origin in God and is therefore to be found where he shows himself to be near and present through his appearances. Whoever is in need of life will attempt to come near to God. Here he knows himself to be in the atmosphere in which life thrives." [103] So it is primarily the meaning and the aim of cultic activity at the holy place, the location of the *deus praesens* ("present God"), to convey "life" to those who take part in the cult. "In the cult the effort is made to preserve life, to strengthen and renew it." [104] So the place in which the cult is celebrated can be called the "fountain of life" from which a "stream of life" flows into the land. The deity itself is the origin and dispenser of life. In this function we come to know the gods of Israel's religious environment.[105] "With great unanimity, the conviction is held everywhere that all life stems from God. 'All life streams from you,' is a confession which belongs to the foundation of every religion. What God possesses in inexpressible fullness, he lets flow down on his creatures." [106]

But it must be asked under what presuppositions and in what sense

[102] Ps. 36:9; Jer. 2:13; 17:13.

[103] Chr. Barth, *Die Errettung vom Tode.* . . , p. 48.

[104] S. Mowinckel, *Religion und Kultus*, p. 63.

[105] That God is "lord of life" is first stated by the Sumerians. The Babylonians characterize Ea, Adad, or Marduk as *bel balati* ("lord of life"). In Egypt Thot is a "treasurer of life." Of Isis it is said: "Her speech is the breath of life." Ptah is called "the lord of life who allows the throat to breathe." Cf. Chr. Barth, *Die Errettung vom Tode* . . . , pp. 37-38.

[106] Chr. Barth, *ibid.*, p. 36.

Yahweh, the God of Israel, is called upon and worshiped as the "fountain of life" in the Old Testament. Upon closer observation and examination it becomes clear that the divine powers in Israel's religious environment are "personifications, hypostatizations, and deifications" [107] of the most heterogeneous natural powers. In the song of Ikhnaton this becomes quite clear. It is the sun, worshiped as a god, which is addressed: "You who gives breath to enliven each of your creatures. . . . If you rise, they live, if you go down, they die. You yourself are the time of life and we live in you." [108] This is an impressive example. In the Canaanite-Syrian religion the gods who dispense life emerge in the revolving seasons of the year: "When the year is over, the world lies in death. New power must be supplied to it, or it must be created anew so that life can live." [109]

But Yahweh is no nature god; the rhythmic events of dying and becoming, perishing and living again do not touch him. He is Lord over life and death.[110] He is a different "Lord of life" from the one worshiped by the people of Israel's religious environment.[111] Three aspects are significant here: (1) Yahweh has demonstrated his life in the history of his chosen people (see above). Thereby he has unmistakably proved his power which stands beyond all natural processes. (2) Israel believed in and worshiped this historically powerful "living God" as the granter of life and blessing. Claus Westermann has clearly shown how varied are the accounts of the "blessing" and the "deliverance" of the God of Israel.[112] But he emphasizes that "this entire, broad and complex area of the blessing was coordinated with the work of the delivering God, with the work of Yahweh, in such a way that the blessing itself became historical or received a historical aspect in which it became that which was promised by Yahweh. . . ." [113] Thus it

---

[107] *Ibid.*, pp. 38-39.

[108] H. Gressmann, *Altorientalische Texte* (2nd ed., Berlin and Leipzig, 1926), pp. 16, 18.

[109] S. Mowinckel, *Religion und Kultus*, p. 71.

[110] I Sam. 2:6; Deut. 32:39; Hos. 6:1 ff.; 13:14.

[111] "He can no longer be only independent development and fulfillment of what man wishes for himself, thus of the ideal self-understanding of a Babylonian, an Egyptian, or an Israelite. Rather, the achievement of the goal set by the Lord of Life has for its content the fulfillment of the promises given by him with life. This goal means for Israel: to be the people called without worth and against its will to responsible participation in the life of God; for the individual: to be a member of this very people (e.g., Deut. 4:20)." Chr. Barth, *Die Errettung vom Tode . . .*, p. 43.

[112] "The blessing or benediction of God happens in an entirely different way from the saving of God; it happens not in the momentary event but in the constant: in growing and thriving, in happiness and success, in achieving greatness and expansion. After its origin, the blessing has nothing to do with history. Its basic meaning is power of fruitfulness which was understood in the whole world of that time as divine power or a power coming from a god." C. Westermann, "Das Verhältnis des Jahweglaubens zu den ausserisraelitischen Religionen," *Forschung im Alten Testament, Theologische Bücherei*, 24 (Munich, 1964), 210. Cf. also F. Horst, "Segen und Segenshandlung in der Bibel," *Gottes Recht*, pp. 188 ff.

[113] C. Westermann, "Das Verhältnis des Jahweglaubens . . ." pp. 210-11.

came about "that Yahweh has become the fountain of life, especially and essentially only in his word and in the prophets, priests, and kings who proclaim and represent it." [114] (3) The Old Testament's theology of creation, with all its complex accents developed in the tradition, determines and forms an understanding of life which stands in clear contrast to that of its religious environment. This understanding of life is incomparable in its radical reference to Yahweh's creative rule.

Thereby the problem of incomparableness and singularity which has been touched upon several times in our study comes up once more.

How can the uniqueness of the Old Testament message be adequately described? Do not even the words and deeds that have no analogy introduce a claim for sovereignty which, as such, does indeed concur with other such claims, no matter how much they differ in detail? [115] Three points must be established concerning this chief question of history of religions research: (1) The Old Testament stands in contrast to its religious environment, not just in "detail," but in its entire structure.[116] Individual aspects can only be properly understood and accented in their uniqueness in the context of the whole event. (2) The singularity of Old Testament assertions has been developed through movements in a long history of tradition, and it must be understood from its history of tradition development.[117] (3) From the antitheses intended in Old Testament assertions, it can be ascertained where the kerygma of Israel distinguishes itself from the religious traditions of its environment and where it wants to be understood under new presuppositions and conditions.

The assertion that Yahweh is "the fountain of life" is properly understood only when these three points are considered. Let us then turn to the decisive passages. At the conclusion of a "judgment speech," the prophet Jeremiah conveys the word of Yahweh:

> For my people have committed two evils:
> they have forsaken me,
> the fountain of living waters,
> and hewed out cisterns for themselves,
> broken cisterns,
> that can hold no water. (Jer. 2:13.)

[114] Chr. Barth, *Die Errettung vom Tode* . . . , p. 44.

[115] E. Käsemann, *Exegetische Versuche und Besinnungen*, II (Göttingen, 1964), 37.

[116] Cf. J. Hempel, "Altes Testament und Religionsgechichte," *Theologische Literaturzeitung*, 5/6 (1956), cols. 259 ff. C. Westermann, "Das Verhältnis des Jahweglaubens . . . ," p. 192: "A comparison of the religion represented in the Old Testament with those surrounding or preceding it can no longer be limited to particulars, but must take totalities into consideration."

[117] Cf. K. Koch, "Wort und Einheit des Schöpfergottes in Memphis und Jerusalem," *Zeitschrift für Theologie und Kirche*, 62 (1965), 291.

For his people Yahweh has continually been, is, and will remain "a fountain of living waters" from which Israel may and should live. But the religious powers of Israel's environment also offer the life-giving element of water.[118] Their offer is, however, both qualitatively and quantitatively of a thoroughly different kind. It is cistern water which seeps out of its cracked containers and lets him who relies on it languish and die.

> All who forsake thee shall be put to shame;
> those who turn away from thee[119] shall be written in
> the earth,
> for they have forsaken the Lord,
> the fountain of living water. (Jer. 17:13.)

What is written on the ground in sand is quickly obliterated. This impressive image stands over against the "preservation of life" which is indicated in the Old Testament with the concept of being entered into the "Book of Life." [120] The ephemeral is placed over against that which endures, power over against weakness, life over against death. The prophets proclaim that Yahweh, as the "living God" himself and in the "most personal way," is "the fountain of life."

Already in Amos an antithesis is established. Not a region nor a cultic center; not a holy sphere nor sacral activity which effects or engenders life—none of these provides Israel with its existence and its salvation. Her God alone does this. Therefore, God's people should not "seek" Bethel, Gilgal, and Beer-sheba (Amos 5:5). Their command is, "Seek the Lord and live" (Amos 5:6). Not the dead local sanctuaries which have fallen under judgment, but the "living God" gives Israel "life." Naturally, this life is, in the first instance, the existence and continuation of Israel in history. But it is more: It is the "good" as such (Amos 5:14).[121] It is a transformation in the sphere of influence of "justice and justification," and therefore, under the dominion of Yahweh, it is standing and moving in the light of salvation.

These first statements in Jer. 2:13; 17:13, and Amos 5:6 refer again to the "living God" who now manifests himself as "the fountain of life" in the history of his people. But the question arises as to how those texts are to be understood which deal with Yahweh as the "Lord of life" in the narrow scope of cultic activity. In the prayer of Ps. 36, the psalmist confesses,

> For with thee is the fountain of life;
> in thy light do we see light (vs. 9).

[118] Consider esp. the Canaanite fertility gods, the baalim.
[119] For the revision, cf. *Biblia Hebraica*.
[120] Cf. Exod. 32:32-33; Ps. 69:28 *passim*.
[121] For the Wisdom context of this passage, cf. H. W. Wolff, *Amos' geistige Heimat*, *Wissenschaftliche Monographien zum Alten und Neuen Testament*, 18 (Neukirchen, 1964), 30 ff.

Vss. 5-9 of this Psalm are of a hymnic character.[122] The words of praise emerge from an "individual lament." They deal with Yahweh's righteousness (vs. 6), with the security that man experiences in the shadow of God's nearness (vs. 7), and with the abundance of blessing that emerges from the abode of the *deus praesens* (vs. 8). All these hymnic assertions flow together in the confession: "For with thee is the fountain of life." From this "fountain of life," which shows its power in such multifarious ways, the one who is praying here awaits deliverance from the powers of his enemies who pursue him, and from the extreme danger into which he has fallen. He is confident that Yahweh will draw him out of the sphere of death and give him "life." Here it becomes quite clear that the power of the blessing of the God of Israel is used with reference to his *delivering* omnipotence.

In Pss. 42:2 and 84:2 there is a similar situation:

> My soul thirsts for God,[123]
> for the living God. . . .[124]
> My soul longs,[125] yea, faints
> for the courts of the Lord.
> My heart and flesh sing for joy
> to the living God.

The *'ēl ḥay* alone is able to supply "life," i.e., deliverance and salvation, to a person who languishes and has fallen into the sphere of death. Yahweh is Lord and fountain of life as he who is present in Israel, in Jerusalem. His power to deliver is witnessed to by the praising and thanking multitude that gathers together for the service of worship at the holy place (Ps. 42:4). Here also the life-giving power of the *'ēl ḥay* is closely joined to his delivering omnipotence.

Thus one sees clearly how, in the cult of Israel, the conception of the "fountain of life and blessing" does not remain related to the natural realm. Rather it receives its own accents through trust in Yahweh's work of deliverance which has proved itself to be powerful and "vital" in Israel (Ps. 22:4).

VI. ὁ θεὸς ὁ ζῶν *in the New Testament*

We have now reached the point where we can observe and investigate in the New Testament the effect of the Old Testament modes of speaking of the "living God." How are the various expressions about the *'ēl ḥay* appropriated in the New Testament scriptures? In which contexts does the

---

[122] For the form historical analysis, cf. H.-J. Kraus, *Psalmen*, I, 281-82.

[123] Revision of the Elohistic part of the Psalms. Cf. *Biblia Hebraica*.

[124] One could also read, "God of my life" (cf. Ps. 42:8*b*), but in consideration of Ps. 84:2*b*, the transmitted text will have to be retained.

[125] Cf. *Biblia Hebraica*.

designation ὁ θεὸς ὁ ζῶν ("the living God") appear, and how is it to be understood?

The best starting point again is the oath formula. The high priest "adjures" Jesus in his trial "by the living God" to tell whether he is the Messiah (Χριστός) (Matt. 26:63). The verb ἐξορκίζειν has the meaning "to make a person swear," [126] "to cause to swear." The facts which were set forth with respect to the invocation ḥay YHWH (Part III) will have to be considered here. Furthermore, an Old Testament quotation (Isa. 45:23) can be ascertained in Rom. 14:11. In Isa. 45:23 the Yahweh speech is introduced by an oath of God which is formulated with the words of bî nišbaʿtî ("by myself I have sworn"). The Septuagint renders the Hebraic text with κατ' ἐμαυτοῦ ὀμνύω. But Paul brings into his quotation the oath formula ḥay ʾānî, well known from the Old Testament, when he introduces the speech of God with ζῶ ἐγώ ("as I live"). Finally, in Rev. 10:6, the phrase "he swore by him who lives" has to be understood in connection with the mode of expression in Gen. 14:19, 22. The explanations of ḥay YHWH given above should here too be considered.

Proceeding now to the designation ὁ θεὸς ὁ ζῶν, we should first refer to the already interpreted quotation of Hos. 1:10 in Rom. 9:26. This is the only place in the New Testament where an Old Testament passage speaking of the "living God" is taken over in its entire wording. Wherever else the designation ὁ θεὸς ὁ ζῶν appears in the New Testament texts, it is found in new, peculiar contexts which we shall now investigate.

Only in Matt. 16:16 (and in the variants of John 6:69) do we find in Peter's confession of the Messiah [127] the wording "you are the Christ, the son of the *living* God." The further, still to be treated passages in which God is called ὁ θεὸς ὁ ζῶν give rise to the general explanation: "Thus at the time of Jesus one called him: the eternal Living One, the living God and eternal king." [128] The Gospel of Matthew, in particular, makes use of this designation (cf. also Matt. 26:63). But the epithet emphatically appended to the confession of the Messiah will bear a yet more specific accent: This Christ is not just any υἱός ("son"), not just any θεῖος ἄνθρωπος ("divine man"), but the son of the "living God" witnessed to in the Old Testament. The reality of his messiahship is confirmed by the reality of the God who attests

---

[126] W. Bauer, *Theologisches Wörterbuch zum Neuen Testament*, under ἐξορκίζω (Stuttgart, 1933 ff.).

[127] Cf. finally: E. Dinkler, "Petrusbekenntnis und Satanswort," *Zeit und Geschichte: Dankesgabe für R. Bultmann zum 80. Geburtstag* (Tübingen, 1964), pp. 127 ff.

[128] See J. Schniewind, *Das Evangelium nach Matthäus*, in *Das Neue Testament Deutsch*, 2 (11th ed., Göttingen, 1964), relative to the passage. Cf. in the Jewish tradition: Jerusalem Berak 3*b*; Jerusalem Sanhedrin 18*a*; Palestinian Thefilla 2; Jerusalem Sanhedrin 16*c*; Tosifta Berak 7:13. In addition, see A. Schlatter, *Der Evangelist Matthäus* (3rd ed., Stuttgart, 1948), p. 504. For the epithet θεὸς ζῶν, cf. also R. Bultmann, *s.v.* ζάω, *Theologisches Wörterbuch zum Neuen Testament*, III, 863 ff.

his living power in Jesus of Nazareth. With Matthew this kerygma of the early community finds a particular emphasis.[129] At the side of the confession of the Messiah in Matt. 16:16 with its emphatic reference to the "living God," one could place in the Gospels only John 6:57 where the concept finds its most pointed expression, comprehensible of course only from the presuppositions of Johannine theology,[130] in the words that ὁ ζῶν πατήρ, the "living father," has sent his son and that the one sent lives διὰ τὸν πατέρα, which must mean: "for the sake of the father." [131] Here the life of the father has entered completely into the son. As the λόγος ("word") he is the ζωή ("life") (John 1:4). "I and the Father are one," says the Johannine Christ (John 10:30).

Specific motives of primitive Christian missionary preaching can be recognized in the only passage of Acts in which the "living God" is mentioned. Those who are addressed in Acts 14:15 are to turn from the vain gods to the "living God." This contrast is known from the Old Testament (see above). The relative clause connected with θεὸν ζῶντα (the "living God") certainly refers also to the Old Testament theology of creation (cf. Exod. 20:11). Yet in vs. 17, in a very far-reaching sense, understandable only from the missionary situation,[132] this very God is spoken of as the "source of life" (cf. Part V). According to Acts 14:15, God proves himself as the "living one" by his deeds of creation and in the patience with which he so far allowed the nations to walk in their own ways (vs. 16).

In the Pauline letters, I Thess. 1:9 is also to be understood from the missionary situation.[133] The context clearly bears this out. The Christians of Thessalonica have turned around, away from the idols to the "living God." Again this contrast has its model in the Old Testament (cf. esp. Jer. 10:10 and the context). Thus, in view of Acts 14:15 and I Thess. 1:9, it becomes quite clear that the Old Testament theologoumenon found a permanent place in the missionary proclamation of primitive Christianity. The pagan gods are vain and dead, but the proclaimed God is "living." In the context of I Thess. 1:9, Paul relates exactly how the "living God" has evidenced his life in the eschatological time of salvation: He raised Jesus from the dead—him, "who delivers us from the death to come" (vs. 10). [RSV reads "wrath to come"—Trans.]

[129] Against Dinkler, I agree with the interpretation that the kerygma of the early community finds its expression in the confession of the Messiah. Cf. R. Bultmann, *Geschichte der synoptischen Tradition* (6th ed., Göttingen, 1964), pp. 275 ff.

[130] Cf. R. Bultmann, *Theologie des Neuen Testaments* (5th ed., Tübingen, 1965), pp. 367 ff.

[131] C. Weizsäcker, *Das Neue Testament* (1937).

[132] Similarly encompassing is the speech of Paul in Athens (cf. Acts 17:23 ff., esp. the strange quotation of vs. 28).

[133] For the proclamation of God in the missions sermon, cf. R. Bultmann, *Theologie des Neuen Testaments*, pp. 71-72.

Twice more in the letters of the apostle Paul, the designation "living God" appears, i.e. in II Corinthians. How this designation is to be understood can be demonstrated first by looking at II Cor. 6:16 and the context of this verse. The apostle explains: "For we are the temple of the living God!" He bases this statement on a quotation from the Old Testament: "As God said: 'I will live in them and move among them, and I will be their God, and they shall be my people' " (cf. Lev. 26:12; Ezek. 37:27). The pledge of the presence of God among his people, the promise of his devotion and covenant faithfulness determine and ground the theologoumenon "living God." But it also determines especially the completely new eschatological situation: that precisely this "living God" is now present in the temple of the bodies of those who belong to him, in the σῶμα ("body") of his congregation.[134] The mode of his living presence is defined in II Cor. 3:3 with πνεῦμα ("Spirit"). Through the "Spirit of the living God" the congregation has become a "letter from Christ," a public letter of recommendation before the whole world. In II Cor. 3, "Spirit" is the "power of the eschatological new covenant." [135] The living God is present in the πνεῦμα. This πνεῦμα is the power which imparts the liberation from the wrath which is to come (I Thess. 1:10) and thereby imparts the justification of faith. It is the δύναμις ("power") out of which the Christ crucified in weakness lives and out of which now the Christians also live in their weakness (II Cor. 13:4).

The designation "living God" also occurs twice in I Timothy. I Tim. 3:15 recalls II Cor. 6:16, yet the ethical admonition now stands in the foreground. At issue is the upright, proper conduct in the "household of God," in the "church of the living God." Where God is present as the Living One, a mode of life corresponding to this fact must be determinative. In I Tim. 4:10, the servants of God are said to set their hope "on the living God," on him who will and shall prove himself the Savior of all men, but especially of those who believe.

It is consistent for the Letter to the Hebrews, which is defined in style and language by the Old Testament,[136] if the designation "living God" appears more frequently in it than anywhere in the New Testament. In Heb. 3:12 we find the admonition: "Take care, brethren, lest there be in any of you an evil, unbelieving heart, leading you to fall away from the living God." God himself is present in the congregation through the "Holy Spirit" who says, "Today, when you hear his voice . . ." (vs. 7). In the φωνή ("voice"), in the λόγος ζῶν ("living word") (Heb. 4:12), God himself

---

[134] In this context, see also I Cor. 3:16 and 6:19.

[135] E. Käsemann, *Exegetische Versuche und Besinnungen*, II, 277. For πνεῦμα as the power of ζωοποιοῦν ("giving life"), cf. I Cor. 15:45; John 6:63.

[136] Cf. O. Michel, *Der Brief an die Hebräer*, Kritisch-exegetischer Kommentar über das Neue Testament (12th ed., Göttingen, 1966), Introduction.

is present and lives in his congregation.[137] Who would be able to turn away from him! In the situation of persecution[138] fearful dangers threaten those Christians to whom the letter is directed. But what is "fearful"? "It is a fearful thing to fall into the hands of the living God!" (Heb. 10:31). No one eludes his judging power (vs. 30).

But the "wandering people of God" of the new covenant is shaped by the saving work of Christ who with his blood purifies "our conscience from dead works to serve the living God" (Heb. 9:14). "*Dead* works" and "service for the *living* God" are contrasted. Christ has made possible and realized this service through the purifying of the conscience, through forgiveness. Through his death he has opened up access to the "living God" and, by this means, a "new, *living* way" (Heb. 10:19-20). Those who have been purified by the blood of Christ and have attained to God through his death "serve," just as do the high priest and the priests of the Old Testament, immediately before the living God.[139] The "priesthood of all believers" is deeply grounded in this event.[140]

"You have come to Mount Zion and to the city of the living God, the heavenly Jerusalem . . . ," Heb. 12:22 says. The wandering people of God already have reached the eschatological goal.[141] The contrast in the context of Heb. 12:22 is peculiar. In vss. 18 ff. the Sinai is mentioned in an antitypical way. But this Sinai is not described in the sense of Deut. 5:26 as the place at which mortal man could hear the voice of the living God and yet live; rather, the roughest sketching out of Exod. 19 depicts the dread in which no man could come near to the mountain. Sinai meant death. But the mountain of Zion, the heavenly Jerusalem, is the "city of the living God," of life for all who arrive at it.

Retrospectively, we can confirm in summary fashion the following about the designation of God as ὁ θεὸς ὁ ζῶν in the New Testament:

1) This designation was familiar in primitive Christianity. In some passages it is clearly pointing to the Old Testament, in others it is alluding to it.

2) This designation was used in the early practice of Christian missions, in order—corresponding to the Old Testament models—to confront the vain, dead gods with the "living God" and thus to attest to the salvation of the turn of life (*Lebenswende*).

---

[137] Cf. here the statements about Deut. 5:26 in Part IV of our investigation.

[138] Cf. Heb. 10:32 ff.; 12:1 ff. See also O. Michel, *Der Brief an die Hebräer*, § 2.

[139] For the significance of Hebrews for the understanding of primitive Christian worship, cf. H.-J. Kraus, "Gottesdienst im alten und im neuen Bund," *Evangelische Theologie*, 4/5 (1965), 178 ff.

[140] Thus O. Michel, *Der Brief an die Hebräer*, with reference to Heb. 10:19-20.

[141] Cf. E. Käsemann, *Das wandernde Gottesvolk*. Forschungen zur Religion und Literatur des Alten und Neuen Testaments, New Series, 37 (4th ed., Göttingen, 1961), and *Exegetische Versuche und Besinnungen*, I, 304.

3) Especially in the Pauline letters and in Hebrews, the epithet "living God" receives new meaning from God's new, eschatological "proof of life," and thereby in the context of the Christ-Spirit event.

VII: *Concluding Questions*

With immediate reference to the last statement we must pose the question: What precisely is the function of God's new eschatological "proof of life" and the specific new molding which the epithet "living God" underwent? Does it take the place of and invalidate all that which is expressed in the Old Testament about the self-witnessing of *'ēl ḥay* in history, about his covenant faithfulness, his constant readiness, his watching, his existence, his strength which bestows life and blessing and his saving power which is also effective for the individual? Has the eschaton taken everything up into a "higher reality"? Is anthropology now the only structure in which the eschatological power of conversion can be appropriately brought to expression, to language? What sense then is there to speak of God? [142]

Must not a new listening to the Old Testament explode the anthropological *incurvatio in hominem?* And in an eschatologically directed ecclesiology, which, if it wants to correspond to the New Testament, can only be profoundly rooted in Christology, must not such a new listening open up a new understanding of the people of God "on the way" of history? And then must not the theologoumenon "living God" be taken up again and recognized in a way that corresponds to its role in biblical theology? Further: What significance does Judaism have as witness of Israel and simultaneously also as witness of the historically powerful rule of the "living God" for theological speech about God? [143] And finally: Does not speech of the "dead God" in all its demythologizing tendencies and existential novel thoughts start with an unbiblical theism or with a high-grade mythological setting? Where is the cry "God is dead!" as passionately uttered as in those old myths which in view of the empirical observation of a desolate and power-depleted reality substitute a mythological analogy for a recondite power?

In which direction will theology go? In the future will it want stubbornly to refuse to listen to and speak to the Old Testament? Will it have a desire to construct with a more or less subtle Marcionism its doctrine of God on the foil of a "biblical-theological" dualism?

[142] R. Bultmann, "Welchen Sinn hat es, von Gott zu reden?" *Glauben und Verstehen,* I (3rd ed., Tübingen, 1958), 26 ff.

[143] Cf. e.g. the sentences of Franz Rosenzweig: "Whether Christ is more than an idea—no Christian can know. But that Israel is more than an idea—that he knows, that he sees. For we live." *Der Stern der Erlösung,* III (3rd ed., Heidelberg, 1954), 199. One thing is certain: Whoever thinks he can pose the question of God without the question of Israel has already taken an ahistorical, metaphysical standpoint.

IV

PAUL'S DOCTRINE OF JUSTIFICATION: THEOLOGY OR ANTHROPOLOGY?*

HANS CONZELMANN

I. Introduction

Paul may still be referred to outside the technical discipline of New Testament study, but he is hardly read. His doctrine of justification is considered to be one-sided and narrow, obscuring the fullness of Christian truth. Furthermore, this doctrine is thought to have nothing to say to our time, precisely *because* it is not in demand anymore.[1] It certainly has never been up-to-date in this sense! The prevalent tendency to try to keep the church standing on its spindly legs with less theology and more sociology, psychology, political science, and of late even "cybernetics," is certainly not new! It is rather a new outbreak of the recurring characteristic tendency of German theology to negate itself.[2] It is, however, precisely when the

* Translated by R. Dick Johns, Tübingen University, from *Evangelische Theologie*, 28:8 (August, 1968), pp. 389-404.

[1] The Lutheran World Federation openly turns away from it and plainly commends the alleged quest of "modern man" for God's existence as such. This is supposed to be more radical than the (outdated) quest for the *gracious God*. Cf. Wilhelm Dantine, "Zum 'Rätsel' von Helsinki," under "Hinweise" in *Evangelische Theologie*, 24 (1964), 45 ff.; and Ernst Wolf in the same vol., under the same title, pp. 48 ff.

[2] Is it accidental that "practical theology" seems determined to take the lead in surrendering commitment to revelation? The most roaring eruption to date occurred in a recent issue of this journal. On the systematic background of the conviction that one gets along better with "less Word" and "more words," see Günther Klein, "Gottes Gerechtigkeit als Thema der neuesten Paulus-Forschung," *Verkündigung und Forschung, Beihefte zu Evangelische Theologie*, 12/2 (1967), 10. He speaks of an ontology, "which receives its concept of the Word from the model of information."

situation in theology and in the church is anything but impressive, that the remedy can only be to get to work, namely, to deal diligently with theology! And this means of necessity, that we have to renew our acquaintance with Paul and, therefore, with the doctrine of justification. The understanding of this theologoumenon is a matter of dispute, not so much among systematicians, but certainly among exegetes.[3] What does δικαιοσύνη θεοῦ ("righteousness of God") mean?

In the attempt to answer this question, we must resist the influence of systematic postulates. The exegete must naturally be prepared to recognize in certain circumstances that Paul and, for example, Luther differ. He must also venture the judgment that perhaps in this instance Paul did not formulate his position clearly enough, that he did not think through all its systematic implications or see all its consequences. He did not construct, of course, a timeless system of doctrine. Every theology is historical. The doctrine of justification, too, cannot be inherited through mere repetition of past positions. There must be new formulations, appropriate to the moment at hand, subject, however, to what Paul and Luther considered a criterion.

The debate about this doctrine is sometimes carried on between the alternative: Theological or anthropological point of departure for Paul? Or, more specifically: Theological or anthropological structure of the doctrine of justification? This terminology can be used as a peg on which to hang our thoughts, if we do not pervert it as a slogan,[4] but carefully define the term anthropology. This terminology is, of course, not completely new. It was rehearsed in another era with characteristic nuances. At that time the issue was "theocentrism or anthropocentrism." [5] We find a characteristic expression of this in Karl Holl's *Gesammelte Aufsätze* (I, 37, n. 2), in an

[3] Cf. The nonchalance with which W. Dantine, in "Rechtfertigung und Gottesgerechtigkeit," *Verkündigung und Forschung*, 11/2 (1966), 68 ff., declares *that* interpretation the right one which is systematically the most acceptable to him, without even mentioning the exegetical facts. See Klein's rejoinder, "Gottes Gerechtigkeit," pp. 1 ff.

[4] This does not provoke thought as much as it elicits associations: One thinks of Friedrich Gogarten, for whom anthropology is a fundamental component of his systematic program; of Rudolf Bultmann, who uses this catchword to characterize an exegetical state of affairs (see below); of Paul Tillich; of Herbert Braun, who enlivened the discussion with his formulation that in the New Testament Christology is the variable and anthropology the constant, in his *Gesammelte Studien zum Neuen Testament und seiner Umwelt* (Tübingen, 1967), 2nd ed., p. 272; cf. pp. 275 ff. For Braun this is apparently not just an exegetical statement, but also a systematic explanation (see also pp. 340-41 and 348 ff.).

[5] E. Schaeder, *Theozentrische Theologie*, Vol. I (Leipzig, 1909; 3rd ed., 1925), Vol. II (Leipzig, 1914; 2nd ed., 1928). Schaeder stands against historicism, which interprets revelation as immanent in history, and against idealism and the sole domination of the viewpoint of salvation in theology. He is *for* the majestic character of God, the understanding of nature and history as the place of encounter with God. Jesus Christ is the "absolute high point and concluding point of the historical mediation of faith in God." See H. Stephan, *Geschichte der evangelischen Theologie seit dem deutschen Idealismus* (Berlin, 1938), p. 278.

essay written in the year 1917. According to Holl, the distinguishing characteristic of the "theocentric approach" is that

the notion of God is not measured by the existence (or "claim") of man. Just the opposite is true. Man is measured by the notion of God. Therefore, one cannot determine what God is by "postulates." But that which is ascertained as regards God presents the "possibility" (or impossibility) for man. . . . Not man's wishes or needs must be regarded as the motivation for religion, but the obligation, the duty placed on us by God.

This is the theocentric point of departure which Holl finds in Luther.[6]

How much the perspectives can change becomes clear when one confronts "theocentric" and "dialectical" theology.[7] For dialectical theology, Holl's beginning point is thoroughly subjective, because the notion of obligation also comes under the category of one's experience of himself.[8] It is apparent that the dispute over "-centrism" was neither abundantly clear, nor was it entirely relevant.[9] It was arranged into the scheme: objective-subjective, *fides quae creditur-fides qua creditur:* God is there—man is here. In this way both were defined by being turned into a *concept.*

"Dialectical theology" questions both positions, the theocentric as well as the anthropocentric.[10] It no longer asks the question, "Does God exist?" It is no longer oriented in a concept of God, world, and man, but in the situation of the entrance of the Word of God.[11]

We proceed from Bultmann's exegetical thesis that Pauline theology is most appropriately represented as anthropology.[12] To understand this conclusion, one must study the course of Pauline interpretation since F. C.

[6] Adolf Schlatter disagrees; his criticism reads, "The exegete (of Rom., namely, Luther) proceeds from his own ego, Paul from God" (*sic!*). *Gottes Gerechtigkeit* (Stuttgart, 1935), p. 38.
[7] Cf. Karl Barth's discussion of Schaeder and Holl in *Kirchliche Dogmatik* I/1.
[8] Karl Holl, *Gesammelte Aufsätze,* III (Tübingen, 1928), 559, written in 1907: It is a generally recognized principle, that "nothing can be acknowledged as valid in religion other than what is encountered as present reality and can be reproduced out of one's own immediate feelings. . . . Also the doctrine of justification must be able to withstand this test if it contains true metal." Cf. Barth in *Kirchliche Dogmatik* I/1, 203-4: This is Cartesian thinking. "Based on this principle, there is no understanding of the Word of God. This is because we neither encounter the Word of God in the reality present to us (but—and this is something different—in the reality present to us it encounters *us*), nor can it be reproduced from our own immediate feelings."
[9] In spite of this, or perhaps because of it, if Schaeder's and Holl's works were presented in a theological lecture today, they would sound very up-to-date.
[10] Rudolf Bultmann, *Glauben und Verstehen,* I (Tübingen, 1933), esp. 1 ff., 26 ff., 85 ff., 114 ff.
[11] Within the group, anthropology soon became the bone of contention. But we cannot pursue this further at this point.
[12] Bultmann, *Glauben und Verstehen,* I, 117-18; see also his article, "Paulus," *Die Religion in Geschichte und Gegenwart,* 2nd ed., IV (Tübingen, 1930), col. 1031.

Baur[13] who prepares the way for a historical understanding of Paul with the aid of Hegel's understanding of history and his conceptual system in two respects: (a) He sees Paul in the context of the entire development of primitive Christianity. (b) He interprets Paul himself primarily from the notion of the *Geist* (according to Hegel, the absolute self-consciousness), and achieves thereby an impressively rounded and comprehensive understanding.

The most important result of the next phase of research is the distinguishing of a twofold conceptuality in Pauline thought.[14] The history-of-religions school pursues this consistently, beginning with the historical derivation of this conceptuality and the different views of salvation expressed in it.[15] It introduces the sociological perspective that a direct comparison of Jesus and Paul is inappropriate. Between them stands the Hellenistic church which determines the position and the views of Paul. The school carries out motif research in which explanation takes place by way of the historical derivation of ideas. The thesis of the twofold conceptuality (the same as the doctrine of salvation) is pursued further. Paul is no longer seen as being primarily the theologian of justification, but as the mystic of being in in Christ.[16] Theology is pushed into the background in favor of "religion." [17]

In a counter-thrust, Holl maintains his position (in strong disagreement with Bousset) that justification by faith is the center of Pauline theology.[18]

---

[13] Albert Schweitzer, *Geschichte der paulinischen Forschung* (Tübingen, 1911), pp. 10 ff. Bultmann, "Zur Geschichte der Paulus-Forschung," *Theologische Rundschau, N.F.,* 1 (1929), 26 ff. Texts edited by Werner Georg Kümmel, *Das Neue Testament, Geschichte der Erforschung seiner Probleme* (Freiburg, 1958), pp. 156 ff.

[14] H. Lüdemann, *Die Anthropologie des Apostels Paulus* (Kiel, 1872) is representative. He proceeds from the thesis that Paul knows a twofold linguistic usage of "flesh," and arrives at the distinction between two different doctrines of redemption, one which is Jewish and juridically subjective, and another which is objectively real. The one is concerned with freedom of the will, law, sin, imputation of righteousness, and faith; the other with the fact that flesh engenders sin and, with it, death as a necessity of nature. Redemption is the overcoming of the flesh. And this second view was actually that of Paul. See texts in Kümmel, ed., *Das Neue Testament*, pp. 235 ff.

[15] Otto Pfleiderer in Kümmel, ed., *Das Neue Testament*, p. 264.

[16] The nature of this mysticism is also controversial: Mysticism of the kyrios cult (the Hellenistic type—Wilhelm Bousset) or objective, sacramental, and eschatological mysticism (Albert Schweitzer)? The anthropological presuppositions remain unexplained. For a critique, see Bultmann, *Glauben und Verstehen*, I, 129 ff.; "Zur Geschichte der Paulus-Forschung," pp. 49 ff.

[17] Wilhelm Wrede's *Paulus* (Halle, 1904) is esp. interesting. It is now reprinted in K. H. Rengstorf and U. Luck, *Das Paulusbild in der neueren deutschen Forschung* (Darmstadt, 1964), pp. 1 ff. In a perceptive analysis, Wrede shows that Paul must be understood as a theologian. But he deplores this, because what is essential for Christianity, in his view, is, in good liberal fashion, the religion of Jesus. Cf. Bultmann, "Zur Geschichte der Paulus-Forschung," pp. 46 ff.; "Jesus und Paulus," *Beihefte zu Evangelische Theologie*, No. 2 (1936) pp. 68 ff., now in *Exegetica* (Tübingen, 1967), pp. 210 ff. Schlatter develops a completely original position in *Der Glaube im Neuen Testament* (Leiden, 1885; 4th ed., 1927) and *Theologie des Neuen Testaments* (Stuttgart, 1909/10; 2nd ed., 1921/22).

[18] Holl, *Gesammelte Aufsätze*, II, 18 ff.

Dialectical theology reacts even more strongly. It gives "theology" a programmatically positive meaning and radically rejects historicism and psychologism which are viewed as partners. Here neither the historical derivation nor the "explanation" of thoughts from individual personality traits are essential to understanding.[19]

When the concept "anthropology" is injected into the exegetical discussion at this point, a counter-program and a program are implied: (a) A counter-program against the "isms" of the *Weltanschauung* era of modern intellectual history, including theology; against positivism which is content with the collection of material; against historicism and its relativizing of the question of truth;[20] against the carrying on of Christianity as a *Weltanschauung;* against the devaluation of history for the sake of a timeless idea. This counter-program was supported by the distinction between decision and resolution, self-understanding and self-consciousness.

(b) The program did not intend to turn a system of philosophical categories into a standard by which to judge. But, with the help of concepts which are well defined and clarified with respect to their presuppositions, it sought to inquire into the appropriateness of Paul's utterances. For example, what does Paul do when he theologizes? Does he sketch, in orthodox fashion, a system of doctrine? Does he, pietistically, give directions for self-illumination? Does he delineate the self-consciousness of the redeemed man?

Bultmann tries to avoid this either/or with his notion of self-understanding, which is disclosed through the Word to faith.[21] He hopes, with Paul's help, to win back the unity of objective and subjective faith, and this not from the side of the believing subject but from the given kerygma, through the understanding of faith as obedience to it.

What can be disconcerting about this program is not the subjective way the question is asked—this is directed precisely toward objective communication—but the amazing agreement between historical exegesis and systematic conclusions. This harmony could be attributed, however, to the consequences of theology's having rediscovered its own original understanding, making possible both, the comprehension of the historical meaning of the text *and* the bridging of the historical distance. Is it not the aim of the text itself to be such a bridge?

If one should then undertake an exegetical examination, the alternative: "mysticism of existence in Christ, or theology of justification by faith?"

---

[19] Emil Brunner says in his comments on Barth's Römerbrief, "Der 'Römerbrief' von Karl Barth," in *Kirchenblatt für die reformierte Schweiz*, 34/8 (1919), 29 ff., reprinted in *Theologische Bücherei* 17, I (München, 1962), 85: "For Paul 'faith' is the grasping of something objective, in which the manner of the grasping is not taken into account."

[20] Bultmann, *Glauben und Verstehen*, I, 1 ff., and 123-24.

[21] *Ibid.*, pp. 262-63. This is the meaning of the disposition of the theology of Paul: "Man before the revelation of πίστις," "Man under πίστις," *Theologie des Neuen Testaments* (Tübingen, 1961), pp. 191 and 271.

still offers a useful clue. Which of the two, then, is authentically Pauline? Or must this alternative itself be overcome? [22]

In a methodological investigation of the text there is interplay between motif history, form history, and tradition history. When in the following a text is referred to under one of these rubrics, it is done for the sake of simplicity. Actually always all methods and viewpoints must be taken into consideration. As we have said, the formulation of the question is two-fold:

a) Mysticism or justification?

b) The meaning of the doctrine of justification itself: theology or anthropology?

II. The Contribution of Form-historical Research

Paul time and again expresses theological claims in the form of quoting a traditional creed and then interpreting it. If a uniform style of his interpretations can be demonstrated, Paul's intention can be comprehended with methodical certainty, as the following examples indicate:

1. I Thess. 4:13-18.[23] In Thessalonica the question arises as to whether those who died before the Parousia of the Lord would participate in eternal salvation.[24] Paul answers by referring to a creed: "For since[25] we believe that Jesus died and rose again. . . ." [26] Then he draws the conclusion for those who believe, "even so. . . ." [27] Thus the statement about Christ is also a statement concerning those who believe.[28] Faith is understood only when it is understood as our destination, when we recognize that our own future is given "in Christ." This is not formally regarded as the future in a general sense, but it is understood exclusively as the future of salvation. The resurrection is not a formal apocalyptic revitalization which is followed by salvation or damnation, but it is entrance to salvation.[29]

---

[22] Cf. Hans von Soden's excellent comments on this in *Sakrament und Ethik bei Paulus* (Marburg, 1931), pp. 1-2.

[23] P. Nepper-Christensen, "Das verborgene Herrenwort, Eine Untersuchung über I Thess. 4:13-18," *Studium Theologica*, 19 (1965), 136 ff.

[24] How the question came up need not be discussed here.

[25] "εἰ" ("if" or "since") is not purely conditional here ("in case that"), but it supposes that this is the case ("if, as it is actually the case"). Paul does not seek to prove the truth of this statement because in Thessalonica no one doubts it. If εἰ is understood causally, this is still not changed.

[26] Parallel passages and linguistic usage here indicate that Paul is quoting. He never uses the word ἀνέστη ("he rose again") when he composes a passage himself. See B. Rigaux, *Les Épîtres aux Thessaloniciens* (Paris, 1956), p. 534.

[27] διὰ τοῦ 'Ιησοῦ ("through Jesus") is to be related to κοιμηθέντας ("those who have fallen asleep").

[28] Bultmann, *Theologie des Neuen Testaments*, p. 192. Rudolf Schnackenburg speaks of "the fundamental Pauline idea . . . : What happened to Christ also occurs to the Christians." *Das Heilsgeschehen bei der Taufe nach dem Apostel Paulus* (München, 1950), p. 152.

[29] H. Schwantes stresses this in *Schöpfung der Endzeit* (Stuttgart, 1963). The next sec-

The anthropological reference of the creed does not append an "application" as something secondary, but it shows that revelation itself has this reference.

2. This same procedure is prevalent in I Cor. 15, once more in connection with eschatology. Is there a resurrection of the dead? Once more Paul cites "the faith," this time in an expanded version (vss. 3-5).[30] Then he expands on the significance of the creed in a daring elaboration: "If there is no resurrection of the dead, then Christ has not been raised." [31] What is implied here is brought out in vs. 17: "If Christ has not been raised, your faith is futile and you are still in your sins." Thus Paul does not appeal to a subjective experience of faith,[32] but to the creed. He does not extract from this creed a mystical anticipation of the future—this is what his opponents in Corinth are doing—but the understanding of faith.[33] His argumentation is not just formal orthodoxy. He begins with the concrete situation of those who have been justified and lifts this situation to the level of their understanding.[34] A formal orthodox argumentation, purely as an allusion to the confession of faith, would be of no value in the discussion with the Corinthians, because they are thoroughly orthodox, in a formal sense. Paul confirms this expressly at the beginning of the chapter. But they are oriented to the terminal point for "faith," the exaltation of Christ which, in their view, annuls his death. Faith and understanding mean for them henceforth the pneumatic stimulation of following the Risen One. Then the point of encounter between Christ and the believer lies in an unreal space. The concrete individual is not encountered, but an ahistorical ideal self. Faith becomes fantastic existence which expresses itself primarily in ecstasy. Historical communal life in the church is dissolving. Paul maintains against this that faith includes within itself a movement which from the

---

tion, I Thess. 5:1-11, serves to overcome the apocalyptic question. The fate of dead non-believers is of no interest to Paul, because his eschatology is not constructed apocalyptically but christologically.

[30] It is generally recognized that Paul uses a formula here.

[31] Here he appears to be arguing with the apocalyptic view of the world, the conception of a general resurrection. In reality, his presupposition is the resurrection of Christ. Also in I Cor. he deals exclusively with those who have died "in Christ."

[32] Herbert Braun's comments in *Gesammelte Studien zum Neuen Testament und seiner Umwelt* (2nd ed., Tübingen, 1967), p. 240, are to the point: Paul does not refer to experience, "he has rather the goal of calling upon the Corinthians to consider critically the presupposition of their belief in forgiveness. If this belief represents only an experience, only a possession of the soul (cf. 4:8), then it is self-deception. Only the essence of faith which is grounded in the eschatological Christ event makes it what it vainly pretends to be as pure experience."

[33] Cf. the frequency of terms concerning preaching and faith in vss. 12 ff.: κηρύσσειν, μαρτυρεῖν ("proclaim," "witness"), etc., πίστις ("faith"). Also of interest is the astonishing conclusion in vs. 56, which (just because it appears so unexpectedly) unmistakably sets a concluding accent here.

[34] This can be used as an illustration of the distinction between self-consciousness and self-understanding.

exaltation of Christ leads back to the cross, from Christ *extra nos* into the world, to the concrete person in his worldly situation. Faith reaches its goal: it comes to every man in his κλῆσις ("calling").

3. Rom. 9:30–10:10[35] joins the creed (10:9) with the theme of πίστις ("faith"), justification, and the end of the law.

4. In Rom. 14:6-12, the conviction "whether we live or whether we die, we are the Lord's" is based on the statement, "Christ died and lived again."[36] We may draw the tentative conclusion that Paul's reaching back to the confession of faith makes it evident that he is concerned with theology and not mysticism. The point of his exegesis is to indicate the direction of revelation and its realization in the world which is understanding in faith. It implies the Word character of the event of salvation, the association of the establishment of reconciliation and the Word of reconciliation (II Cor. 5:19).

This intention is even more clearly prevalent in two further instances:

5. Rom. 3:24-26.[37] We accept Bultmann's and Käsemann's supposition[38] that a formula lies behind this passage which deals with the justice of God as a being just (θεοῦ, subjective genitive).[39] God is just and shows this through his gift of Christ as an expiatory sacrifice.[40] The effect of this deed is the elimination of sin committed "before." This means, interpreted objectively in forms of the history of salvation, sins committed until the death of Jesus and the establishment of the new covenant. Subjectively, it means until a person's entry into the church and, therefore, until baptism.[41]

Paul interprets this in the following way:

a) He introduces the formula with vs. 24 and places the accent on "grace alone."[42]

---

[35] See below under "δικαιοσύνη θεοῦ"; Günther Klein, "Gottes Gerechtigkeit," pp. 8-9.

[36] ἔζησεν is, of course, an accommodation of an ἐγήγερται, or ἀνέστη to the intention of the context. A further interpretative element here is the κύριος title.

[37] The question of the meaning of δικαιοσύνη θεοῦ will be discussed later.

[38] Bultmann, *Theologie des Neuen Testaments*, p. 49; Ernst Käsemann, "Zum Verständnis von Römer 3:24-26," *Zeitschrift für die Neutestamentliche Wissenschaft*, 43 (1950/51), 150 ff., and now in *Exegetische Versuche und Besinnungen*, I (Göttingen, 1960), 96 ff.

[39] "Righteousness" here can mean (in the sense of Jewish linguistic usage) God's being faithful to his covenant. But this is not certain. It can also be understood as his distributive justice.

[40] On ἱλαστήριον (expiation), see G. Fitzer, "Der Ort der Versöhnung nach Paulus, zur Frage des 'Sühnopfer' Jesu," *Theologische Zeitschrift*, 22 (1966), 161. As the title indicates, Fitzer suggests the translation: "place of reconciliation."

[41] There is no reflection here on sins after baptism. The person who is baptized now stands in the new covenant.

[42] Bultmann and Käsemann assume that already the basic element in vs. 24 belongs to the formula. Paul is supposed to have added the passage, "by his grace as a gift." But their different analysis does not alter the basic point of our discussion.

b) He adds "by faith." [43]

c) He supplements the formula in vs. 26 by repeating its main point and then interpreting it in his own way: "It was to prove . . . that he himself is righteous," i.e., "at the present time," and "he justifies him who has faith in Jesus." Therefore, the "proof" of God's justice does not lie in the past. It occurs today, that is, in the proclamation of the gospel (cf. Rom. 1: 16-17). God is righteous in the sense of proclaiming or making one righteous.

Paul's theological style is clear: Christology and soteriology coincide in the Word character of the event of salvation.

6. Rom. 4:25. The diction here shows pre-Pauline elements.[44] Paul otherwise does not connect resurrection and justification. His style is apparent in the exegesis of this formula from 5:1 onward, word by word: "We are justified" (the same verbal style of speech about justification as in Rom. 3:21 ff. and 26) "by faith" (cf. the τῇ πίστει in vs. 2) "we have peace with God." [45] The interpretation of the new existence in the world amid temptations follows. The triad faith, love, hope constitutes a guiding theme. The statements are permeated again and again with allusions to the confession of faith (5:6-7, 8, 10). The entire section Rom. 5-8 can be shown to be a commentary on the creed, as considered from the aspect of justification by faith.[46]

7. Rom. 6.[47] The statement that Christ (has died or) was "buried" and raised from the dead is of further service to Paul as the basis for his interpretation of baptism.[48] The interpretative element here is the preposition συν- ("with"). This is considered one of the strongest proofs for the presence of a second, sacramental, "realistic," doctrine of redemption.[49] But here συν- is used neither in a mystical nor a magical sense. What Paul is aiming at becomes apparent when one begins with the formula upon which it is based. One is tempted to draw the conclusion:[50] Therefore we have

[43] That this is an addition is apparent from the fact that it cannot be meaningfully related within the sentence. It marks Paul's intention as a kind of exclamation point.

[44] Concerning the word παραδιδόναι ("he was given over" or "put to death") in formulas, see K. Wengst, *Christologische Formeln und Lieder im Urchristentum* (Bonn dissertation, 1967), pp. 50 ff. Cf. Rom. 8:31 ff.; Gal. 1:4; Isa. 53:6, 12. Joachim Jeremias refers to Isa. 53:5b, "he was bruised," in "Das Lamm, das aus der Jungfrau hervorging," *Zeitschrift für die Neutestamentliche Wissenschaft*, 57 (1966), 215. Whether this parallelism is to be conceived of as being synonymous or synthetic, cannot be absolutely decided.

[45] O. Kuss, *Der Römerbrief* (Regensburg, 1957), pp. 200 ff., returns to the reading ἔχωμεν (instead of ἔχομεν). He notes, however, that this will not determine the total view of Romans.

[46] The circular composition of chaps. 5-8 leads back to the creed. This flows into a comprehensive description of existence in the world (8:31 ff., 35 ff.).

[47] N. Gäumann, *Taufe und Ethik* (München, 1967).

[48] *Ibid.*, pp. 61 ff. Romans was written a short time after I Cor. (15:3-5 ἐτάφη ["he was buried"]).

[49] On the terminology, see Gäumann, pp. 32 ff., and on the problem, pp. 134 ff.

[50] The Corinthians were actually tempted to do so.

died and been raised with Christ. Paul shatters this direct analogy between the redeemer and the redeemed ones (in a way that is harsh even language-wise) by changing over to the future tense: the resurrection still lies ahead of us.[51] Up to this point we will find ourselves "in" Christ in καινότης ζωῆς ("newness of life"), the freedom of a new way of life.

Although between the beginning of Rom. 5 and the conclusion of Rom. 8 the concepts of justification recede, Paul presents no other doctrine of redemption than he advances earlier and further on, since this section cannot be detached from the passages which bracket it.[52] The eschatological proviso (in chap. 6), the doctrine of justification, and the theology of the cross have the same meaning.

III. Conceptual Analysis of δικαιοσύνη θεοῦ

The current controversy is associated primarily with this concept.[53] Paul can speak of God as being righteous by appropriating Jewish (Rom. 3:5; 9:14) and early Christian (Rom. 3:25-26, see above) parlance. This kindled the dispute over the question of whether the genitive θεοῦ ("of God") with δικαιοσύνη ("righteousness") should not be understood exclusively or at least preferably as the subjective genitive. But we should not get caught up in the formalities of grammar, particularly since some of the usual classical classifications no longer apply. We must also count on the possibility that Paul's own linguistic usage, as is true of most of his concepts, is not consistent.[54] Here, too, the anthropological test can be of decisive methodological service. The leading question is how the relation of God and man is determined by this concept. Upon what is man supposed to focus?

Decisive is the observation that the rare subjective sense of the genitive appears consistently in the tradition. Where Paul picks up this tradition, he interprets it, without exception, in a new way. He flatly rejects the question of God's being righteous (Rom. 3:5-6), and the positive early Christian

[51] The uses of the future tense in Rom. 6 may not be minimized as being "logical." Paul is consistent on this point. Cf. in vs. 8 the pattern πιστεύομεν ("we believe").

[52] N. Gäumann, pp. 158 ff.; E. Lohse, "Taufe und Rechtfertigung bei Paulus," *Kerygma und Dogma*, 11 (1965), 308 ff.

[53] The originator of this is Schlatter. The latest literature includes: Ernst Käsemann, "Gottesgerechtigkeit bei Paulus," *Zeitschrift für Theologie und Kirche*, 58 (1961), 367 ff., now in *Exegetische Versuche und Besinnungen*, II (Göttingen, 1964), 181 ff.; Eberhard Jüngel, *Paulus und Jesus* (Tübingen, 1962), pp. 17 ff.; Christian Müller, *Gottes Gerechtigkeit und Gottes Volk* (Göttingen, 1964); P. Stuhlmacher, *Gerechtigkeit Gottes bei Paulus* (Göttingen, 1965); R. Bultmann, "ΔΙΚΑΙΟΣΥΝΗ ΘΕΟΥ," *Journal of Biblical Literature*, 83 (1964), 12 ff., now in *Exegetica* (1967), pp. 470 ff.; Günther Klein, "Gottes Gerechtigkeit als Thema der neuesten Paulus-Forschung," *Verkündigung und Forschung*, 12/2 (1967), 1 ff.; K. Kertelge, *"Rechtfertigung" bei Paulus* (Münster, 1967).

[54] Heinrich Lietzmann in *Handbuch zum Neuen Testament*, Vol. III, *Die Briefe des Apostel Paulus*, Part 1, "Einführung in die Textgeschichte. Der Paulusbrief an die Römer" (Tübingen, 1919), pp. 91-92 on Rom. 10:3.

utterance about God's righteousness he transfers to the verbal claim of his δικαιοῦν ("justifying," see above). This means that where Paul takes up this concept, he deals with *my* righteousness, given to me solely through God's grace. This is also apparent from Paul's consistent tie-in of the concept of justification with the concept of faith.

Two characteristic stylistic features are conspicuous here:

a) The verbal style (Gal. 2:15 ff.; Rom. 3:21 ff.; 5:1 ff).

b) The christological transposition of the concept (I Cor. 1:24, 30). The use of the verb δικαιοῦν ("to justify") allows one to discern where Paul starts in his thinking. Actually he begins with the subjective quest for salvation, with the question of how one fulfills the condition of salvation, of how one can attain righteousness which is valid before God.

1. Gal. 2:15 ff. (cf. 3:8, 11, 24; 5:4):[55] "our endeavor to be justified."[56] The anthropological style appears in the verbal style, in the transition into the first person singular, in the association of justification with the notions of faith and of judging. Finally, it is apparent in the fact that Paul draws anthropological statements out of the Old Testament (Gen. 15:6, with the catchword λογίζεσθαι, "to reckon," or "to impute";[57] 18:8; Hab. 2:4; Lev. 18:5).

Naturally man's need for salvation is an objective condition for Paul. This is precisely the reason he can begin here when he deals with justification. The individualism appears even more clearly when one compares this passage with Rom. 9:30 ff. (see below). There Paul speaks in a similar manner about *Israel's* search for righteousness. The collective and the individual aspects can be interchanged.[58]

2. Rom. 3:21 ff. presents a similar situation. After the theme of God's righteousness is formulated in Rom. 1:16-17 and prepared for by the theme "God's judgment"[59] in 1:18 ff., it is thematically handled here. The goal of the section concerning the "wrath of God" is the statement in 3:20 (cf. Ps. 143:2; Gal. 1:16), which is another verbal formulation. The transition to vs. 21[60] is typical. The supplementary phrase "apart from the law" shows that "the righteousness of God" is transferred to man. Then it leads straight in the same direction: "The righteousness of God through faith . . . for. . . ." This is the authentic definition of this concept by Paul. It also moves in the same direction as the formula discussed above and the exegesis of it. From

---

[55] On the difficult vs. 17, see G. Klein, "Individualgeschichte und Weltgeschichte bei Paulus," *Evangelische Theologie*, 24 (1964), 126 ff.

[56] Gal. 5:4: "you who would be justified by the law," i.e., who *want* to be justified.

[57] Cf. Rom. 4:8-9 (Ps. 32:1-2).

[58] Cf. G. Klein, "Individualgeschichte und Weltgeschichte bei Paulus," pp. 126 ff.

[59] ὀργή ("wrath") is not an affect of God, but judgment. Cf., the expression "day of wrath" in 2:5 and the exchange with κρίμα ("judgment") in 2:2-3. See further I Thess. 1:9-10. Paul does not expressly say that God is wrathful.

[60] In this νῦν ("now") is hidden the temporal moment of the reference to the historical revelation; cf. vs. 26.

behind light is shed once again on the genitive θεοῦ ("of God") by the expression "all have sinned and fallen short of the glory of God," i.e., the glory which is appropriate to God.[61]

As a control test we may add that from the consequences which Paul describes in vss. 27 ff., there are no lines leading back to a subjective interpretation of the genitive.

3. Rom. 1:16-17. This is the key passage for the "subjective" interpretation which refers, among other things, to the corresponding genitives connected with (εὐαγγέλιον), δύναμις, ὀργή (["gospel"], "power," "wrath"). But this reference does not really settle anything—"gospel" and "righteousness" are not parallel here. The gospel is the mode, righteousness the content, of revelation. And the "wrath" of God stands parallel to righteousness only in a formal sense. The decisive difference, that judgment is not revealed in the Word, is essential. Judgment is not the content of a message which is communicated, but a manifestation from heaven. Paul also does not speak of God's power "subjectively," because the content of the good news is not "wrath and grace." Since it is exclusively gospel and transmission of justification, Paul knows no isolable power aspect of God (which was of so much concern to "theocentric" theology).

The reference to God's power cannot be separated from the more exact designation, "for salvation to everyone who has faith," and therefore, from the anthropological point.[62]

4. As Paul defines the righteousness of God as the righteousnes of *faith* in Rom. 3:22, so he explains in Phil. 3:9 the entire phrase, and especially the genitive:

a) τὴν διὰ πίστεως Χριστοῦ

("that which is through faith in Christ")

b) τὴν ἐκ θεοῦ δικαιοσύνην

("the righteousness from God")

Each is prepared for by refusing its opposite, which is striving after *one's own* righteousness, and this means, justification through the law. Here, too, we find a characteristic association with verbs of judgment (ἡγεῖσθαι and γνῶναι) [from the passages "I count everything as loss . . ." and "that I may know . . ."] and the anthropological reference which is apparent from the dative case.[63]

---

[61] One can confidently paraphrase this: "which is valid before God" or "which they should have with God." Similar genitive constructions are in II Cor. 1:12. On the relation of "glory" and "righteousness," see J. Jervell, *Imago Dei* (Göttingen, 1960), pp. 180 ff.

[62] The Pauline dative! An isolation of "power" consistently leads to faith becoming a formal submission. God becomes the numinous. And in the decisive moment faith is left without the Word. Faith thereby becomes, however, a subjective act of the free will (which could be described as the hidden central dogma of modern, confession-conscious Lutheranism).

[63] a) γνῶσις, γινώσκειν, εὑρεθῆναι ἐν αὐτῷ, δύναμις τῆς ἀναστάσεως, κοινωνία παθημάτων, συμμορφίζεσθαι ("knowledge, to know, to be found in him, the power of

119

5. In Rom. 9:30 ff.,[64] Paul summarizes biblical passages cited. He begins once more verbally: the Gentiles have *not* pursued righteousness. With Israel it is different, but, in any case, "it is not enlightened," since it sought righteousness with the help of the law.[65] This is clarified by showing that the Jews did not understand *God's* righteousness. He explains what this means by using the same counter-concept as in Phil. 3:9, i.e., one's own righteousness. Pursuing it means denying obedience to God's righteousness.[66] Therefore, they have not accepted the *proclaimed* righteousness of God.

If δικαιοσύνη ("righteousness") appears as personified in the following dialogue, it is not, of course, the "righteousness of God," but the righteousness of *faith*. There is no difference between the two, but Paul prefers to work with this explicative expression because it presents the antithesis to the justification based on the law.[67]

6. II Cor. 5:31 speaks for itself. A discussion of the attempt to inject here the subjective genitive is superfluous.[68]

IV. Motif-historical Analysis

The style of the transformation of the concept of "the righteousness of God" can be still more clearly described. Especially in I Cor. Paul works with ideas of (Hellenistic-) Jewish wisdom.[69]

Jewish theology declares that God is wise. This means:

a) (God's) *Being* is wisdom.

b) Man can obtain wisdom from him alone.

---

his resurrection, to share in his suffering, becoming like him");

b) δικαιοσύνη, νόμος, πίστις ("righteousness, law, faith"). The first list has no mystical meaning: "Knowledge" has a communicable, understandable content. "To be found" means to be judged (Gal. 2:17; II Cor. 5:3); it is commented on in the phrase beginning "not having. . . ." The second list of concepts is decisive. Even "to become like him" is not mystical union. It has the same meaning as "to worship in the spirit of God" and "to glory in Christ Jesus." See H. D. Betz, *Nachfolge und Nachahmung Jesu Christi im Neuen Testament* (Tübingen, 1967), p. 146.

[64] On Rom. 10:6-10, see M. J. Suggs, " 'The Word Is Near You': Romans 10:6-10," *Christian History and Interpretation,* Festschrift for John Knox, ed. by W. R. Farmer and C. F. Moule (Cambridge, 1967), pp. 289 ff.

[65] In the phrase "as if it were based on works," the word ὡς ("as if") refers to the subjective nature of the striving.

[66] See the thought connection from 9:30 by way of vss. 31 and 32 (πίστις), to 10:3 and 4 (εἰς δικαιούνην, cf. vs. 10); and once more the dative cases!

[67] The personification here is in the style of the Wisdom literature.

[68] Cf. Adolf Schlatter, *Paulus der Bote Jesu* (Stuttgart, 1934), pp. 568-69.

[69] In many places the hypostatizing of wisdom is still dimly visible, although in Paul it is already diminished to a large extent (perhaps already in the Jewish school tradition in which he grew up?). There are connections with all three Jewish types of hypostatized wisdom: Hidden wisdom (I Cor. 2:6 ff.), wisdom which has disappeared (I Cor. 1:18 ff.) and wisdom that is near (Rom. 10:5 ff.). Concerning these types, see B. Mack, *Logos und Sophia* (Göttingen dissertation, 1967). Wisdom also stands behind other conceptual expressions: ἀλήθεια ("truth," III Esra 4:34 ff.), ἀγάπη, δικαιοσύνη ("love," "righteousness").

1. Paul takes up this association of thought in I Cor. 1:18 ff. and "translates" it: *Christ* is God's wisdom (1:24). That this redefinition is not solely a rhetorical formulation, but a systematic thesis, is apparent from its extension to other concepts of God's manifestations: δύναμις ("power"), then in vs. 30, δικαιοσύνη, ἁγιασμός, and ἀπολύτρωσις ("righteousness," "sanctification," and "redemption"). The genitive is paraphrased once more by the use of a preposition, ἀπό ("by"). Thus from the traditional, objectifying assertions about God, his nature and governance, Paul makes statements about the way God reveals himself "in Christ" and in the gospel. The agreement with the passages already discussed is indicated once more in the factor of judging (2:2) and in the use of the dative.[70]

Thus we are confronted with a consistent individualization. Only the individual can decide. Faith liberates him from his original collective—Judaism, paganism (and analogously today, Christianity or non-Christian religion)—and confronts him with the gospel.

Christ, of course, has not become the wisdom and righteousness of God "for us" just because we acknowledge him as such. We can only do this because this is what he really is. Faith discloses this very insight.[71]

The christological transformation of these concepts is the key to the meaning of δικαιοσύνη θεοῦ: Christ is God's righteousness—for those who believe.[72]

2. Perhaps Paul's boldest thinking as to his focusing of the gospel on the individual is reflected in his analysis of the "I" in Rom. 7:7 ff.: "I was once alive apart from the law, but when the commandment came, sin revived and I died" (vs. 9). When, where, how? Clearly, this is not a report about an inner, subjective experience, but a subsequent judgment of faith about one's own past, because as a sinner, as one who has died, I cannot experience myself at all. Rom. 7 portrays how, in the moment of the awakening call which comes from without, I come to know myself. Faith is the possibility of seeing myself from outside myself. Here also Paul works with categories of Wisdom: What he describes is existence in Paradise and its loss, in other words, the story of Adam, which he transfers to the "I." Thus the objectification of the history of salvation is completely dissolved. Revelation is verified in the individual.[73]

[70] Ulrich Wilckens esp. refers to this in *Weisheit und Torheit* (Tübingen, 1959), pp. 21-22.

[71] To nonbelievers the cross *appears* to be folly because it *is* folly, God's folly.

[72] Further examples of the reshaping of wisdom: I Cor. 2:6-7; 11:2 ff.; 13.

[73] Rom. 7 introduces a wide-ranging complex of themes: predestination and freedom, bondage of the will and personal guilt, fate and theodicy. These themes can be understood, when they are carefully worked through anthropologically, as the truth of faith which I can exemplify in myself, in having my sins literally behind me in the hearing of the justifying Word. In this hearing of the Word, I know that I have been possessed by my sins and could not free myself from them.

3. In the interpretation of the *spirit,* the relation of individualization, freedom, and the individual's ties to the community is clear. Paul develops his concepts in the polemic against the enthusiasts in Corinth, who try to "sell" the spirit as a subjective experience. They cultivate spiritual self-edification. In religious excitement the pneumatic ascends to heaven—let the fellow Christian see to it how he gets hold of the same powers. Possession of the spirit is demonstrated in the practice of freedom, over against the powers of the world, the gods, and the σάρξ ("flesh"), that is, in libertinism. It is no contradiction to this when one notices that the contours of the human personality are dissolved by these religious enthusiasts. In religious eperience the individual merges with the totality of the spirit (in theory with the exalted Lord). The Lord is no longer the crucified Jesus of the kerygma, but in fact a projection of the pneumatic self-consciousness. The congregation is no longer the community of believers, but a collective, which exists in the loss of selfhood, in a fantastic self-consciousness.

It is well known what Paul brings up against this, namely, the confession of the Lord (I Cor. 12:3) and the wider meaning of the χαρίσματα ("spiritual gifts") to cover every contribution toward the building up of the congregation. *Everyone* has a χάρισμα ("charisma"), and everyone has his very own. Each person has, not freedom in general, but his very own freedom in the historical community. That "in Christ" one is no longer Jew or Greek, slave or free, man or woman, is not an enthusiastic but an eschatological statement. Paul does not deny or ignore the political, social, or even the physical differences, but he explains that "here," in Christ, in the church, they are *invalidated.* They are of the order of the world, and not of the order of salvation. This statement interprets existence in no other way than the one, which asserts that God meets everyone in his κλῆσις ("calling"), and thus acknowledges man apart from any accomplishment on his part.

4. This same style of thought can be demonstrated in other themes: The recasting of the understanding of history (Rom. 9–11),[74] the interpretation of the tradition of the Last Supper, the doctrine of original sin and inherited death, the comparison of Adam and Christ. All these themes become transparent only when they are interpreted as the elaboration of the understanding of faith.

This is not only true of Paul, but of any theological statement really well constructed. The test question, posed by the content of the gospel itself, is whether in my theological reflection I remain in my place, that is, in the world, as a sinner who has been declared just, and whether I thereby do

[74] The ideas of Rom. 9–11 remain speculative (not for Paul, but for any reception today), if they are not verified in our existence in the church. Barth tried this in his day in his *Römerbrief.* Schlatter protested against this: "Karl Barth's 'Römerbrief,' " *Theologische Bücherei,* 17, (1962), 144.

justice to revelation itself. One can also say, whether in every theological claim the *sola* (*sola gratia, sola fide*) is taken into account. If this is labeled a subjective criterion, so be it. In any case, it is not a subsidiary criterion appended to the Credo as an application, but it is posited in the Credo itself. The clarification of the anthropological criterion is nothing other than the methodical attempt to understand theology as theology of the cross, or, what is essentially the same, to take justification into consideration. The application of this criterion can lead to freedom for proclamation, since it leads out of the hopeless alternative of whether the preacher has an obligation to objective dogma or to subjective conviction.

V. Conclusion

The present situation can be characterized, on the right, by a tendency toward a renewed objectification and, on the left, by a subjectivizing tendency with a strange mixture of intellectualism and emotion, a kind of intellectual pietism. And—the extremes meet. Fundamentalism needs, in order to express itself, a manipulation of psychology and *Weltanschauungen* which takes on strange forms because it lacks intellectual substance. But— "theology after the death of God" is still preoccupied with the objectifying question of whether God exists. In order to get a grip on "modern man," it also brings in elements borrowed from *Weltanschauungen,* down to the latest faddish follies, logistics and cybernetics (follies not in themselves but as "theological" aids).

Of course, proclamation does not have to preserve the language of yesterday.[75] Its essential point of orientation, however, is not "modern man"— a product of abstraction—but the sinner to whom God persistently reaches out. Proclamation should not seek points of contact in feelings of sinfulness, cosmic threats, or other anxieties. Instead its task is to make contact on grounds of the capacity of the Word. Faith is not a remedy for every possible problem, nor is it a way to fulfill every wish. The objective situation of man is disclosed through faith. This situation is determined by the cross.

Neither objectivism nor subjectivism offers a criterion for present-day ethical problems and decisions. Fundamentalism can easily acknowledge the atom bomb as protection of the church and declare the reintroduction of the death penalty a Christian duty. A *formal* insistence on the "power" of God willy-nilly will slip into some kind of analogy of worldly power. And a theology without God corresponds to an unhistorical, spiritual, or pseudo-spiritual way of thinking. What should we do? We can only recommend that more intensive attention be given to the doctrine of justification as the article of faith by which theology stands or falls.

[75] One cannot refrain from remarking that whenever theology wants to be supermodern, it "discovers" the great thinkers of the past and their language.